Wild Road Home

for the wild –
Christina
Oct 1, 2017

Praise for Christina Nealson

Drive Me Wild: A Western Odyssey
Colorado Book Award Finalist
La Femme de Prose Quill Award Finalist

"Once in a while a book leaps out at you for its sheer energetic force. Nealson's memoir, *Drive Me Wild: A Western Odyssey*, does just that."

– *The Taos News*

"The feminine energy espoused in *Drive Me Wild: A Western Odyssey* is surpassed by none. Christina Nealson brings us on an incredible journey to reach one conclusion: we must preserve, embrace the beauty and respect nature, the earth and all of its connectedness. For these reasons she has been chosen *Focus on Women Magazine* Author of the Year."

– Joslyn Wolfe, Publisher

"...there's a lot of wisdom here: 'Why,' she wonders, 'was it some pushed back and others pushed over, content with the status quo?' And she's certainly no pushover herself: whether she's facing a mother bear and her cubs or the painful reality that her marriage may be in trouble, she always jumps in with an adventurous spirit and an open heart. A soulful account of Western vistas..."

– *Kirkus Reviews*

"*Drive Me Wild* is an odyssey about the wonders of this planet, the vicissitudes of a marriage, the wild heart of many places. It is a mixture of great joys and deep sorrows. There are whales, dolphins, mountain lions, moose, sea turtles and grizzly bears... even a miraculous gastrolith! This is a lovely book, a lyrical disquisition on a very complex journey, told in simple and crystal-clear prose. It is crammed full of delights, beautiful country and sudden little miracles. Diamonds of experience and information glitter on every page. Turn in your badge, Jack Kerouac, there's a new sheriff in town and her name is Christina Nealson."

– John Nichols, *The Milagro Beanfield War*

"This book's a wild ride, a deep story, a journey that will open your heart and prompt your soul to speak. It's not easy, but no real journey is. It is beautiful and funny, scary and sad, honest and compelling. It pairs words we often think of as antithetical: "motorhome" with "enlightenment," "aging" with "power." Read it and be swept away."

– Susan Tweit, *Walking Nature Home*

Living on the Spine:
A Woman's Life in the Sangre de Cristo Mountains

"Her work is not a linear portrayal of the facts but rather a poetic and reflective glimpse of the heart and soul. It is gentle, gracious and profound."

– *Library Journal*

"Christina Nealson is the West's answer to Annie Dillard, yet Nealson's voice is so authentically her own. This is a book of eloquent witness to questions that cannot be answered, only lived."

– Julia Cameron, *The Artist's Way*

Also by Christina Nealson:

At the Edge: Cooperative Teachings for Global Survival

Living on the Spine: A Woman's Life in the Sangre de Cristo Mountains

New Mexico's Sanctuaries, Retreats and Sacred Places

Drive Me Wild: A Western Odyssey

Wild Road Home

Memoir of an Adventuress

Christina Nealson

Wild Road Home
Memoir of an Adventuress

A Wildwords Publication

Printed in the United States of America

*****

Credits
Photos by Christina Nealson
with a nod to the Utah wildscape.
www.christinanealson.com

Formatting and cover design by Debora Lewis
www.arenapublishing.org

*****

ISBN-13: 978-1974465729
ISBN-10: 1974465721

these words are dedicated to roots

flesh and flora

the source of all

Grandmother Tree
where this quest was born

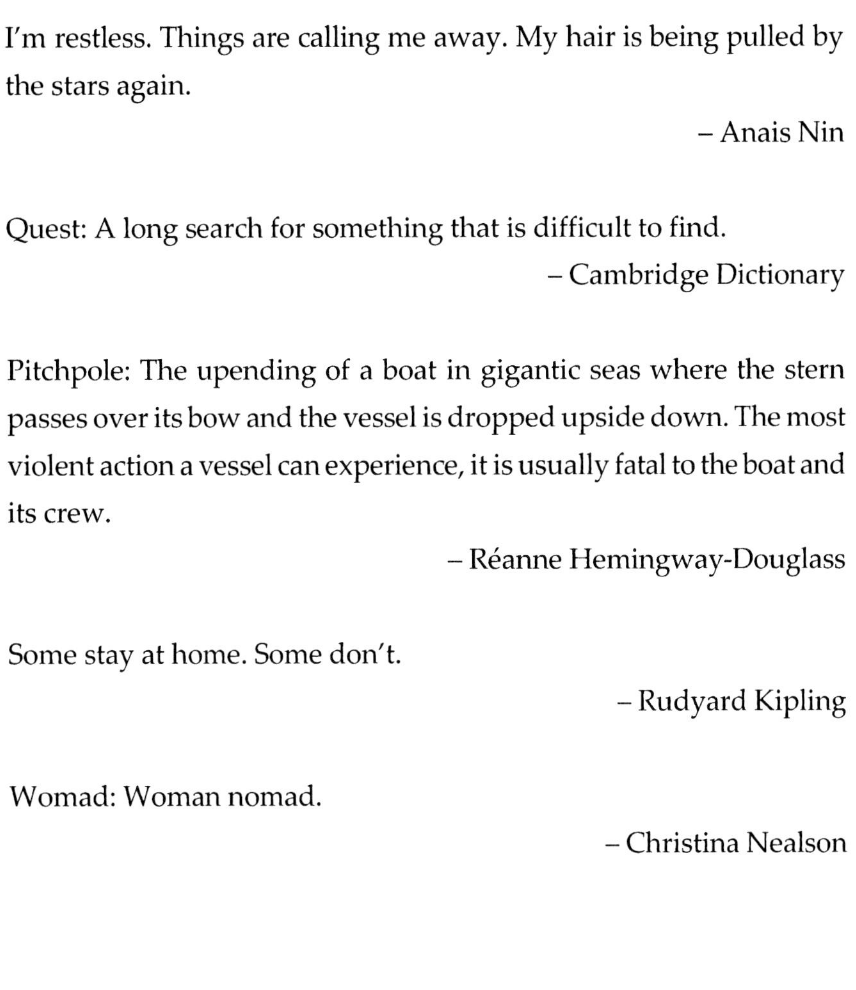

I'm restless. Things are calling me away. My hair is being pulled by the stars again.

– Anais Nin

Quest: A long search for something that is difficult to find.

– Cambridge Dictionary

Pitchpole: The upending of a boat in gigantic seas where the stern passes over its bow and the vessel is dropped upside down. The most violent action a vessel can experience, it is usually fatal to the boat and its crew.

– Réanne Hemingway-Douglass

Some stay at home. Some don't.

– Rudyard Kipling

Womad: Woman nomad.

– Christina Nealson

Prologue

If frenzy had a color it would be blood orange. Six days before my Alaska departure I'd scribbled my name across divorce papers, cashed CDs and traded my foxy Toyota truck for a trailer-towing V-8 Ford. Beauty for brawn. Yes, blood orange, like the fiercest sunset, incinerating the past to make way for a new day. I emptied office drawers into packing boxes and stepped onto the balcony. Distant Sharkstooth Peak jabbed the cerulean sky. I glanced at the boxes and back to the peak. No contest. I headed into the Colorado high country.

The air was eerily warm for early June. Up, up I climbed, through the virginal green of new-leafed aspen; across rushing streams of snowmelt and meadows lush with marsh marigold. I emerged into the barren expanse above tree line, exposed. Ah yes, there it was again, that invincible woman-alive feel. I eyed the twelve-thousand-foot saddle and climbed on. With a hundred feet to go, the trail disappeared under snow. I stepped gingerly across the sun-softened drift field, almost across, and whoosh! — I fell through to my crotch. A Zen smile etched my face. Mountains were ripe with metaphor. I plunged my hiking stick to the earth, leaned and lifted; polished off the steep slope.

I set my soggy self below Sharkstooth's craggy point; beheld familiar peaks south to New Mexico and west to the Sangre de Cristos. I opened my water bottle, gave the first drink to the mountain and took a swig. Then I stood and faced northwest, in silent salutation to Alaska and the nameless future before me.

Quests have no itinerary. I didn't know if my tracks heading north would be there to follow when I returned south. Perhaps, like this day, they would melt into the earth, diminutive amidst nature's grandeur. Of this I was certain: Quest is little about reaching the door and everything about walking through the doorway. Stripped of the roles and rituals born of habit, one travels naked as a newborn. Light and darkness shape the shadows, illuminating the way, one holy, hell-bent step at a time.

Part One

Siren Song

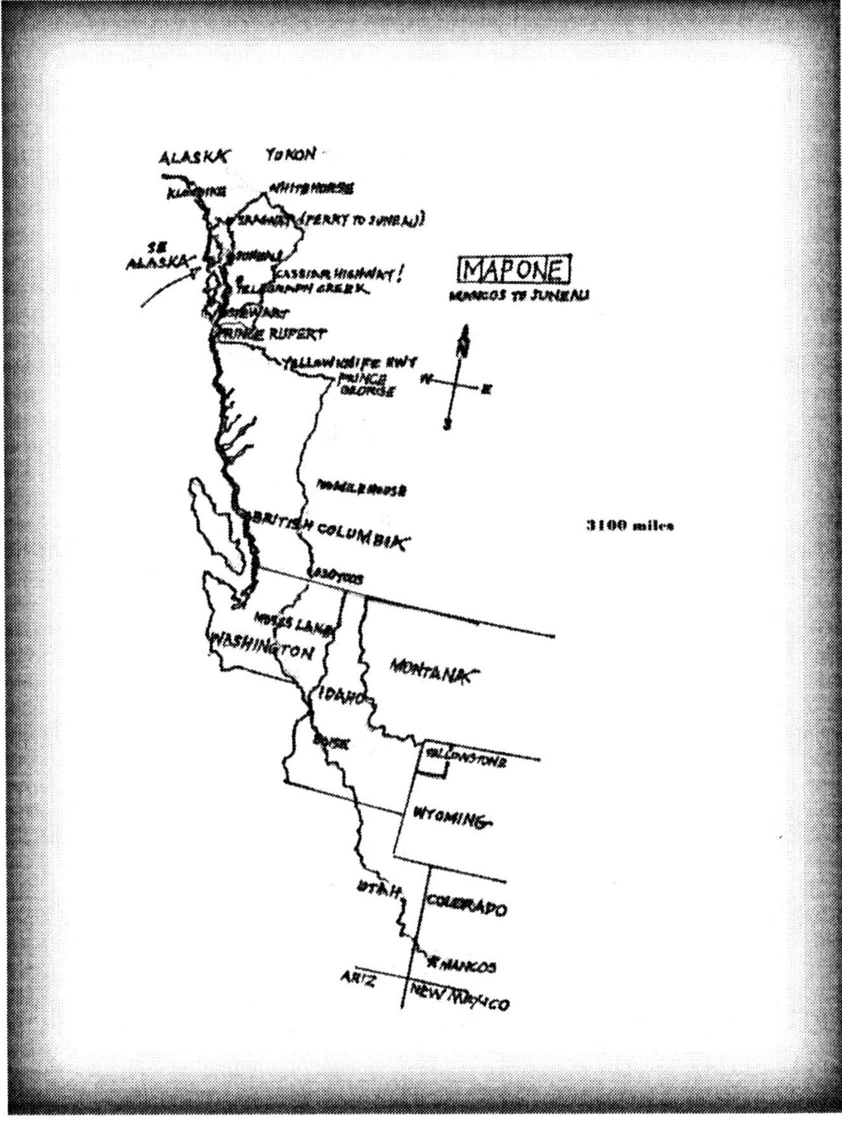
ALASKA
YUKON
SE
ALASKA
CASSIAR HIGHWAY!
MAP ONE
MANCOS TO JUNEAU
PRINCE RUPERT
PRINCE
GEORGE
BRITISH COLUMBIA
3100 miles
WASHINGTON
MONTANA
IDAHO
WYOMING
UTAH
COLORADO
MANCOS
ARIZ
NEW MEXICO

Our fight split the air with a prophetic snap. No couple got away with a trip to the Eiffel Tower devoid of a tingling tongue kiss. Yet there we were, Jay and I, hurling accusations atop the most romantic icon on earth. Our bitter words tumbled onto Paris rooftops; littered the walkways of Luxembourg Gardens. I'd heard the *SNAP!* all right, but denied the doom. I surrendered to inertia and hoped that things would change. It took five years to reach this day of reckoning; to move through the tangle of emotion and excuse. To see my way clear to the freedom road.

Thunderheads roiled to the west as I packed the woman wagon, a nineteen-foot glistening white travel trailer affectionately named La Perla – the Pearl. Pooka watched intently from the tall grass that lined the lane. She'd lived her life on the road with Jay and me. Traveled fulltime from British Colombia to the tip of the Baja, crisscrossing the West. The spotted cat knew the rituals of departure and waited for the signal to jump aboard. The Bengal didn't know she was staying put. I cast my voice to her hiding place and delivered a prayer and a promise: *Take care, little one. I'll be back for you.* She'd be happier with her cat door into the hay mow than on the waters off Alaska. I couldn't look her in the eye. Couldn't have seen through the tears anyhow. I was already dreaming of her.

How long would it take to put a decade and a half in the rearview mirror? Dread and excitement reeled me far from center. There were nights I awoke in panic, swung my feet onto the floor to ride out the groundswell. Moments when I wondered what the hell I was doing. I'd had the ideal little day job, administrator of the local visitor's center. I was surrounded by a heart-full community of friends and a landscape of wildspeak – trails known to my feet, a family of birds and flowers. Now here I was, set to ditch income, take solo to the road, and all I could say was *It's not time to settle down.*

Get 'er done I muttered. There I was again, boxing up routine. I didn't know why ordinary life eventually felt like a barred cell. My astrologer, in her *fait accompli* voice, attributed it to my Libra sun, Aries moon and Sag rising. I credited my tomboy spirit nurtured outdoors by a vivid imagination. I pointed with certainty to genetics, generations of strong-willed, independent women whose DNA congealed into jail keys. Especially notable was my flight from a comfortable married life in Boulder to build a cabin at the edge of wilderness, but I was forty then. Now I stared down sixty. Healthy, yep. No meds, no aches or pains, no physical complaints, my hair still brown and long. I was headed to Alaska to answer a once-in-a-lifetime invitation.

I'd met TAM – The Alaska Man – nine months earlier while winter RV-ing on Lake Havasu. After thirty-five years in Alaska he was yanking up roots and returning to the Lower 48. It was now or never if I hoped to make it out to sea with a seasoned guy-guide. It also didn't hurt that my buddy had a body of steel and a cute smile that dampened my inside thighs. He was quintessential wilderness man. I savored the chance to see the wild through his eyes. He said he wanted to explore islands and show me a special far-away tree. If it was a line, it was a good one.

Three-thousand miles to go. Giddyup! *¡Ándale!*

I walked slowly around the truck and trailer; a methodical check to make sure the hitch was secure, vents closed, stairs up, signals worked. One more glance to Pooka's hiding place, a turn of the key, and Teak and I edged slowly up the gravel road toward the highway. Teak perked up in the backseat as her Lab-brown eyes sparkled: *Oh boy, road trip!* For me, a gut-wrenching mile to the stop sign and a right turn west onto Highway 160. The manic confluence of woe and liberation.

Teak leaned intently against the window, following her olfactory map until familiar territory ceased. White lines disappeared below the front bumper as I wondered what the mileage marker would read when I'd traveled beyond the dead zone of divorce. How far to the thrall of terra infirma? *A ways, Sister. A ways.*

La Perla the Pioneer (Woman) travel trailer towed flawlessly. Blue, the automatic transmission Ford F-150 truck, performed with pizazz. The Colorado-Utah highway was littered with Jay-familiar turnoffs and campsites from our fulltime RV life. I cried the memory bank clean for six asphalt hours. Skipped the ice cream I'd promised myself in Moab and sped right past the entry to Arches National Park. The gas gauge forced a stop in Price, Utah, where Teak leapt from the truck, took the bare minimum of steps and squatted to pee. I reminded her, as I did every day, that she was the best dog in the world.

Azure skies turned charcoal as we started our lengthy descent toward Salt Lake, a curvy mountain route I'd traveled a dozen times. Sprinkles soon gave way to hefty raindrops, whereupon the sky opened, unleashing hail and horizontal rain sheets. The wipers couldn't keep up as I began the steep decline. I turned on the emergency blinkers and slowed to a crawl. I looked to pull over but a construction zone had turned safe shoulders into pockets of thick deep mud. Forced to continue, I white-knuckled it 'round mountain curves.

Down the mountain I crept, piercing headache and all. I hit a straightaway, fled the hydroplane highway and pulled into a Walmart parking lot. I'd eschewed their free offer to dry camp for years; this day I didn't think twice. I swerved into the outer fringe of pavement, crawled from behind the wheel, unlocked La Perla's door and fell exhausted onto the bed.

I awoke at nightfall, one eye at a time. Teak jumped from the floor beside me as I let out an ol' yehaw! I roughed-rubbed her ears and said I'd be right back. I grabbed my purse and headed for the big box florescent innards, strode past the gray-haired greeter with pink lipstick and emerged with a pint of rum raisin ice cream. Teak and I ate the whole damned pint as the thrill of new life eked its way into my psyche. *Here we are, Teak. Wha' d'ya say*? Her ears perked; she tilted her head with joy. Ya, she could get used to ice cream every night. Hold the raisins.

Darkness fell as security lights filled my sleep room with high noon glow. I pulled my blindfold and ear plugs out of the drawer. Instant dark and quiet, safe and sound. I slept deep until dawn, slowly roused by a dog's cold nose on my arm and the muted heckle of Laughing Gulls from the tops of light poles.

Freedom was palpable until I hit the bathroom. One glance in the mirror and I froze, as memory pounced on the afternoon I had stood before the same mirror and watched myself pull the gold diamond wedding band from my finger. Jay had put the brakes on our five-year motorhome odyssey; a travel web tapestry we'd spun like happy-drunk spiders from British Columbia to the tip of the Baja. But while his brakes engaged in a desire for a house and job in one place, mine failed. I'd hit my soul stride adventuring the back roads – writing, taking photos, nudging into remote silent places and communing with the wild. I wasn't ready to stay put in one place, with or without him.

Five years into the fulltimer life I'd perfected the RV-rag, seamlessly melding electric, propane and solar systems. I was enlivened with the transition to La Perla and the autonomous, debt-free life that came with it. The cozy cabin was a perfect place to write. I was, wink, a-loft on wheels: nine nighttime steps from the queen bed on one end to the toilet on the other, the galley (kitchen) and door in between. To the right of the walk-around bed was my altar, special objects that roused memories, inspired insight. Muse fodder: candles, sage and sweet grass, a dinosaur gastrolith, precious feathers and stones, a fist-sized quartz crystal and tuner. To the left were my .357 Ruger and my silent, ergonomic, multi-speed vibrator. Be prepared! The Girl Scout motto never died.

I exited the highway near Moses Lake, Washington, toward an enticing lake and wetlands. The gravel road suddenly narrowed. Bumps got deeper as I willed the map to deliver on its promise of a parking lot by water. More nervous by the second, I shifted into 4WD, rounded a sharp curve and gunned it up a small hill. I called it quits on a tight dead-end loop by a small dam; exhaled thanks to the level spot next to cascading water.

I leaned my head against the top of the steering wheel. I'd just headed down an unknown road towing my life behind me, trusting instinct and my ability to deal with whatever might happen. There was no one to rescue me, no one to share the failure or success of my choices. I was scared witless. I was euphoric. And I was danged certain I'd just passed through the doorway.

I donned camera and binocs and started down a faded path along water's edge. Teak's happy tail pointed to the sky. I stopped every few feet to glass the water and reeds, overjoyed at my welcoming committee – Yellow-headed and Red-winged Blackbirds, Eastern Kingbirds, a Great Snowy Egret, Cinnamon and Blue-winged Teals,

Northern Shovelers, Coots, Phalaropes, White Pelicans and Northern Harriers. A carrot-colored sunset painted the western sky. Bits of cobalt blue poked from a lone gray cloud. A solitary fisherman walked the distant shore. A poetic vision or a possible threat, I was ever aware of what moves. I watched until he disappeared, retired to Perla and tucked myself in.

I awoke the next morn with dreams of Zimbabwe's Victoria Falls, no doubt spawned by the rushing water over the little dam. I lay in bed and recalled "Smoke that Thunders" – the name the Matabele peoples gave the deadly falls on the Zambezi River. While the rainbow-studded mists were magnificent, it was a bull elephant that had stolen the show as he sauntered down the middle of the village street and scattered terrified locals like pool balls. Jumbo owned the market as he stepped up to an abruptly-deserted vegetable stand, wrapped his trunk around a fifty-pound bag of oranges and methodically lifted it into his mouth. After several minutes he reached into his mouth with his curved trunk, extracted the nylon net bag, dropped it onto the dirt street and continued on.

I lay back with journal, pen and a dreamy smile. My MO was clear: chew and savor. Extract the remnants, lay them to rest and amble on.

Morning espresso bubbled through the stovetop Bialetti as I turned the pages of *Milepost*, "the bible of North Country Travel." At 800 pages, this book covered every Alaska-Yukon-bound road north of the Lower 48 and described them mile by mile. There weren't that many roads across the Canadian border but they stretched a hell of a long ways with sparsely-situated gas stations. I would need to know where they were. This book brimmed with details, coveted maps and advertisements of local tourist traps, RV parks, hostels, mechanics and helpful photos. It didn't, however, prepare me for $8.00/gallon gas.

My scheme was to solo half the way up British Columbia to Prince George and turn toward the coast to Prince Rupert, whereupon I'd take the Cassiar Highway, the furthest-west, off-the-beaten-route to Alaska. Tam had offered to hop a ferry and travel south to Prince Rupert and make the final leg of the trip with me. He'd never traveled the Cassiar and relished the chance. We'd travel together to his home in Juneau. Fair enough. I'd visit him four to five months and leave with winter's threat. Alas, departure would come sooner, on the cusp of changing winds not coupled to weather.

Teak and I closed in on the Osoyoos border crossing and the red wind-furled Canadian flag. My upbeat hello was met with a terse line of questions from the border agent that ended with *Ma'am, deposit that lettuce into the trash or we will fine you. It will be the most expensive head you've ever had.* I bit my lip to keep from giggling, tossed the lettuce into the garbage bin and sped north. Forests soon enveloped us. My transition from sand to moss was under way. The Chihuahua Raven's call would soon be echoed by the humongous Alaska Raven's, perched upon a Sitka Spruce.

The road, my therapist. No co-pilot chatter to pass the time, just the silent allure of solo. Travel was initiation. No matter the purpose or mode, miles and landscapes, it changed me. This was true when I hopped a bus at age seventeen, Chicago-bound during the riotous 1968 Democratic Convention, and it was true when I hopped on a plane in my late thirties bound for Antigua, Guatemala.

I knew no one and did not speak Spanish. The Government effort was under way to annihilate the Mayan population. State Department travel advisories warned tourists away. And yet, I went. Once immersed in the power and splendor of the Mayan cosmological world, I answered the call to photograph the mothers of the disappeared, their sons and daughters kidnapped in the night and never seen again.

It marked a titanic transition in my life. Out of touch with friends and family, years before the internet, I learned to trust the unfolding of events and my capacity to handle what was presented. I wonder if such an initiation is even possible today, in this time of instant connection and GPS-trackers. One can be solitary but not cut off for long.

70 Mile House, 100 Mile House. That's how the town signs read as I journeyed north. Road weary, I pulled into a visitor's center at 150 Mile House and hiked around a worn lake path. I attempted to unlock Perla's door to perk an espresso and it wouldn't budge. Locked out, I secured Teak and headed to the visitor's center to borrow a ladder. It wasn't long before I drew a crowd. Smiling meekly, I climbed the leaning ladder and slid a window open. Heave ho, I pushed myself through the twelve-inch opening, tilting shoulders, flailing legs and all. Thank you, morning yoga. Thank you, mind that forgot to lock the window. Wander Woman here didn't ask for help, which made the climb tougher but ultimately more satisfying. Until I discovered, once inside, that the door wasn't locked. It was stuck. All I had to do was to grab the bottom and give it a hearty yank. Perla had a healthy dose of coyote.

It was roughly five hundred miles to Prince George, where I would turn west and repeat that mileage to Prince Rupert. Tam's arrival by ferry put me under the gun. With the rare exceptions of mechanics and funerals, I had avoided timelines my first five years of travel. I was anxious to move beyond the nondescript towns of lower BC, but there wasn't time to go far afield except at night when I departed the highway to boondock. This was escapade time: miles into mountainous territory, following intuition up unshouldered forest roads. Once parked, I hiked, threading my way through ominous piles of grizzly bear scat. I no more returned and closed the door and mosquitoes darkened the screens. Daylight waned but never surrendered to darkness as I fought to keep the glass half full. I was ready to put southern BC behind me, excited to see Tam and head *North to Alaska*. Kept humming that song.

Teak and I walked along the oceanfront, watching for the Alaska Ferry. The last time I had seen Tam was early spring in Utah. I'd been his tour guide as he passed through Moab, introducing him to the smooth red rock country that rimmed the Colorado River. Our time was short and it had been hard to say goodbye. We'd talked often by phone, moving our friendship along. I looked forward to seeing him again. Alaska land, sea and flesh-scapes waited. I was confident, with Perla my escape hatch. I had my own space and what could go south in a mere four months? Besides me?

People on foot were the first to debark. I anxiously sought his familiar face. Yes. There he was, The Alaska Man, carrying a black duffle bag, smiling like a sixteen-year-old. A long warm hug, a few pats for Teak and we were on our way, ahead of the long ribbon of cars about to unfurl from the bowels of the boat.

The Cassiar Highway stretched 450 miles from the Yellowhead Highway east of Prince Rupert, B.C., to the Alaska Highway in the Yukon Territory. Along this narrow stretch of blacktop were access highways west to intriguing places like Stewart Hyder and Telegraph

Creek. I was about to witness mountain peaks and glaciers of mythical grandeur. I wondered if I would catch a glance of the Kermode bear (KerMOdee). "Spirit Bear" to the natives, its coat white or cream. The Kermode was thirty percent more effective at fishing in the daytime than its dark bear cousins due to its light coat and pale reflection on the water.

Tam and I headed up the highway, catching side glances at one another like two shy kids. There were streams or rivers around every curve, with myriad access roads and private places to boondock. Our desire led us to a sweet spot by a stream, surrounded by wildflowers. We stepped outside to confirm our "O ya, it's perfect" feel ... followed by the social science signs of foreplay: wide smiles, lengthy eye contact, tight hug. Then Tam turned away and began to rummage through his duffel bag. Voila! – he handed me a pair of knee-high, weighty boots called Xtra Tuffs. Okaaaaay. I kicked off my sneakers and slipped into the glass slipper, er, Xtra Tuff. It fit perfectly, as he explained he'd sized them with a friend named Erma, who also wore a six-and-a-half. Some women get sexy négligées, I got brown neoprene waders with felt liners.

I set up the innards of the trailer, unpacking the breakables out of travel mode, as Tam grabbed his fishing rod and strode upstream. "We don't call it catching," he winked. But for him, it *was.* The man was phenomenal. Depending on the stream or lake, he returned with trout, grayling or pike. And never just one. He filleted like an artist, prepared the secret coating and fried them up. Nothing sexier than that.

A loon and four mergansers floated outside the window as we shivered, entwined and touched one another toward ecstasy. Neon purple exploded across my brain as I came to him again and again. I was back. No more questioning if long-gone desire was because of the ex, age or hormones. No more fearing I was forever high and dry. Tam and I rolled side by side and broke out in hysterical laughter. The tickles and banter were on: *Ooooo ya, welcome to Alaska Man's Fishn' Fuck Tour*. We laughed our way to utter silence. My body spent, a woman returned to herself.

That night, a dream. Tam introduced me to a woman at a party. I liked her; then realized that she and Tam were married. In spite of the revelation, a friend of Tam's encouraged the two of us to get together. Tam was sympathetic and understanding toward me, but I felt trapped. With his wife present, and his divided attention, it was impossible for us to be with one another.

I awoke with questions. Would I be trapped by his ghosts? Was there another woman? The dream portrayed someone else in the picture and my dreams often foretold the truth of relationships early on.

That evening, as we sat by a small campfire, I asked if there was another woman in his life. Yes, he said. Liz and he had been together seven years when she slammed the door and left for good, tired of alcohol-infused arguments. He said it was over. He meant Liz. Not the drinking. There were ripples on the water as we closed in on Dease Lake. I felt unsettled in the land of constant light; wore a blindfold to seal in sleep.

Lakes dotted the roadside like a string of glassy pearls, spattered with loons, Barrows goldeneye and ducklings that zipped at mom's command. We were far enough north that Alaska was to the west. In fact, Juneau was due west, over impenetrable mountains. We dropped the trailer at a campsite and trucked west toward the Pacific, down a seventy-mile stretch of gravel road with twenty percent winding grades. Destination: Telegraph Creek, a ghost town from Klondike Gold Rush days.

The route followed the Stikine, a river so spectacular that John Muir described it as "a Yosemite a hundred miles long." The road leveled off along a narrow volcanic promontory with four hundred foot drops on both sides. A few dozen horses rounded a curve at roadside; a ghost-like arrival out of nowhere. I walked amongst their muscled magic, stroking the receptive mares as a fierce-eyed stallion looked on. It was he who determined, after a few minutes, that we were done, as he tossed his wind-whipped mane and herded his harem away. They disappeared as quickly as they had materialized. I smelled my hands; blew horsehair into the air.

We descended the no-guardrail switchbacks to the Stikine into a deserted village of dilapidated houses. Bright yellow. Turquoise. Hot pink. I was enthralled. I jumped from the truck, camera in hand; missed the handwritten "keep out" sign.

Spirits were palpable. I proceeded reverently around the vacant homes. Shabby chairs dotted porches. Whiskey bottles hung from roof gutters. Homes were adorned with moose antlers and rusted crosscut saws. Sheds of vertical jack pine logs peppered the lush lands situated between river and cliffs. Slightly larger than New Mexico's *latillas*, the vertical slats were a couple of inches apart.

Suddenly, a bent-over Indian man appeared. I feared we'd overstepped an undiscernible boundary, akin to entering an off-bounds pueblo kiva. My apologies were ready but the crusty man let loose with a toothless grin and said hello; pointed to my camera and asked if I had noticed the eagle cliff. I smiled back and told him I'd seen two bald eagles calling to one another. He waved me to follow and pointed to a gigantic rock face that lined the confluence of the Stikine and Tahltan Rivers. A wind-etched eagle with outstretched wings adorned the cliff. Perched directly over the etching was a Bald Eagle, perusing her domain. My new friend said that their nest was up there. He extended his hand and said his name was Donny. His weathered face told a thousand tales. He reckoned that he was glad to have some company.

Donny's Tahltan tribe would gather soon below the eagle face when the salmon returned from the ocean to spawn and die. Donny had already caught a few Chinooks (Kings) and Reds (Sockeye). We followed him to a pine house and stepped inside. I was Alice down the rabbit hole, witness to rows of orange filleted salmon, hanging vertically to dry on horizontal wooden poles. Sunlight burst through the slats of the tangerine world, a sacred salmon sanctum, as Donny climbed into the loft, reached into a bag and handed down some dried, smoked salmon. I took a bite of dried fish that could only be called divine. I chewed slowly and savored as Donny descended the ladder and offered salmon eggs on the end of his knife. Roe. His caviar.

Donny continued to walk with us and excitedly shared his stories. Then, as suddenly as he had appeared, he stopped; said he had to go. I thanked him; said we were continuing on to Telegraph Creek and asked if he needed anything. He said no as his eyes beamed with simple truth: he had all he needed in this place where rivers converged. Our goodbye handshake was like a prayerful clasp. When I turned to wave a final goodbye, Donny was gone.

Telegraph Creek was quiet and empty as Tam and I walked up and down the short main street. Most of the 350 year-round residents worked for the Tahltan First Nations Peoples, or in tourism, logging and construction. The view downriver was much the same as in 1800s gold rush days; the timeworn buildings spoke of bygone days at the edge of the world. It was a seven-day trip downriver to Wrangell and the Pacific, a journey that conjured images of Bogart and Hepburn on the African Queen. Pure adventure; hold the leeches. We grabbed a burger and a cup of java, then headed to the truck. I wanted to return to Donny's village.

Donny wasn't in sight as I walked up to his little blue house. I left a signed copy of my book, *Living on the Spine,* against his door. My heart to his.

The further north we ventured, the more wild the terrain. Four black bears in one day. Thirteen total thus far. I collected wood and struck a match, ever aware of the four elements: fire to warm; earth, smattered with trails of moose scat; air's evening gush of mosquitoes; water simply everywhere, in this land of gray-green wet. Clouds and waterfalls threaded down steep mountainsides for miles. Humidity eased my southwest-sun wrinkles, smoothed my sandstone-dry feet. I'd met no one with tanned brown skin like mine. My days of lying naked in the sun were far, far away.

Day brimmed with energetic wonder, night delivered peace. Sunset was no longer an event for which I rushed to grab my camera to catch a few moments of glowing sky. I sat lakeside for hours and watched blue hues turn rose. Fell trancelike into the glistening water trails of ducks. Soft satin light did not die in this authentic twilight zone.

We joined the Alaska Highway at the BC/Yukon border just west of Watson Lake. We passed through Teslin, Johnson's Crossing and Jake's Corner and turned south toward Atlin on gummy roads that spewed mud like spitballs. I didn't get the upshot until we stopped to camp and I couldn't open the door. La Perla was La Negra.

It was a damp camp. Rain had turned the earth to puddles and soaked the firewood. Tam headed out to fish as I sat at shore with my journal. Bald eagles were prolific. Their chirpy cry had fixed deeply into my psyche since my meeting with Donny. A side trip to Google had revealed that the basalt rock formation so cherished by Donny was known as Sesk'iye cho kime, or Home of the Crow. The trickster, so I had read, was regarded as the creator of light who helped bring humans into the world. The rock represented the birthplace of the Tahltan. I couldn't help but wonder if Donny, with that sly look in his eye, was the ultimate trickster.

Rain held off as we continued our string of charmed camping spots. Tam hooked grayling and pike. At his behest, I donned my boots and occasionally cast lines with the pro. The little RV freezer overflowed. We ate his fare with wine accompaniment. Gin and tonics were apropos. I couldn't get enough of his hunting stories – grizzly encounters and excursions with bush pilots into Alaska's mountain wilderness. When done with his day he took out his hearing aids and fell into bed, leaving me with quiet time to read and write. Or ... not. Combing sex tangles from my hair was a new pastime as a sista's words rang true: the best way to get over one man was to get under another one.

We crossed the border between British Colombia and the Yukon four times before arriving at Alaska U.S. customs. The fifty miles to Skagway was a dramatic, cloud-shrouded descent lined with barren tundra-like rock and pools. I imagined Skagway a quiet village at seaside studded with Klondike Gold Rush broken dreams; Main Street memories littered with gun fights and shenanigans. I expected to hear the ghosts of madams calling through alleys.

It didn't happen. The highway that entered from the north was a straight shot to the ocean where my gaze stopped at a colossal cruise ship. From Skagway's deep, mountain-studded harbor came up to ten thousand shoppers a day onto the Disney-esque boardwalk, into the hands of t-shirt shops and diamond sellers that beckoned like car salesmen. The snazzy jewelers had no reason to be there. The diamonds were not mined locally, any more than they were mined in Juneau and Ketchikan, other port towns that had sold their souls to cruise ship companies. The ship companies were instrumental in setting up these stores and had financial interest as they plied their captive audiences with want. It was a genius marketing sleight of hand. The new gold rush. I couldn't catch the ferry to Juneau fast enough.

One could not drive to Juneau. The glacier-covered Coast Mountains ensured her isolation. It cost $300-plus to board myself and forty-two feet of truck and trailer as Tam climbed aboard without reaching for his billfold. Now retired, he was once a bosun on the Alaska Ferry System. As the senior crewman of the deck department, he had been responsible for the ship's hull. He now had the privilege of riding the not-so-cheap ferry for free, and I couldn't help but wonder why he didn't offer to drive Blue and Perla onto the ferry at no charge. A question I should not have ignored.

It was one hour to Haines and another four hours south to Juneau. I stood at the rail. Humpback whales dove and sky-hopped; Jaegers fell from the sky in dramatic dives for gulls; Marbled Murrelets skimmed the water in pairs. Yes, this was why I came to Alaska. I couldn't wait to board Tam's boat for island adventures. To full-on feel the land of wild wet.

We departed the ferry womb into Juneau's coastal gray. My brain lurched as I encountered a string of fast-moving cars. Juneau was my first city since Boise. Home to around thirty thousand folks, it was a thin strip of humanity at the base of major avalanche chutes. Steep mountains rose at the backside. Mountain goats grazed high above homes. Water was everywhere – lakes, streams, cascading falls and ocean. Fog fell gently on my skin as mist. I had traveled from 7500 feet to sea level; from lands that rarely lose the sun to lands that receive rain 222 days a year.

We inched up a hill in a nicely groomed trailer park and pulled into Tam's drive. I couldn't wait to see his house, unhitch Perla and settle in. Tam tossed me my boots instead. Alaskans did everything in these boots 'cept make love. And that was only a guess. It took a half day clad in rainwear to power wash the mud and squashed bugs off Perla. Her white returned as the dirt of remote places ran down the street in a thick brown river. Washed anew. Ready for the reckoning.

Can't keep Perla in the driveway said Tam. *She's too big. And you can't stay in Perla, neighborhood rules.* It took a few moments to register: I was moving in with Tam. Hold it right there. I was several weeks out of a marriage and moving in with a man? Friend with benefits? Rebound man? Whatever he was? Underwear in 'my' drawer (his dresser). Jeans on 'my' hangars (his closet). Oh Lordy, this wasn't going to do. And Perla, my home and writing space, parked blocks away, on a vacant lot.

Confusion reigned inside the confines of Tam's home. I'd not only lost the sun, I'd lost my protocol. I didn't do TV or news in the morning. He did. I didn't have internet access on my computer. He did. I preferred silence with my morning stretches. He didn't. Like silence or stretches. To top it off, the trailer park neighbors were so close that the windows were covered. I was trapped in a man cave, surrounded by pictures of people from his past.

Our first intense words were in the kitchen. He couldn't believe that I could leave such a mess when I prepared anything. I didn't see a mess. For fifteen years I didn't *have* to see it. I cooked and Jay cleaned up. That was our deal.

The rain fell continuously as soggy bumper stickers asked "Got Wood?" Another proclaimed "Alaska Welcomes Global Warming." Ravens floated haunting bass calls across Sitka spruce as Tam and I watched the weather report, willing a swath of sunshine. Meanwhile, I plied my host with his first green chile cheeseburgers and red chile pork stew, cool weather comfort foods that branded me a Southwesterner. The Alaskan took venison from the freezer, sliced it into strips and fried it up in a homemade batter to die for. *Where did you shoot the deer* I asked, fixing to hear another Alaska story. *In the head* he answered.

I was eager to meet Herb, a classic Alaska outdoorsman and revered friend with whom Tam had shared many hours at sea. He prepped me as we neared the house: *Herb's full of a million stories, one of the classiest guys I've ever known. He pokes fun at himself all the time and hardly ever makes bad remarks about anybody, but if he doesn't have any use for you he won't put on airs.*

Tam had met Herb shortly after his arrival in Juneau. A whippersnapper following his dream, Tam needed work and Herb hired twenty-something Tam to work at his transfer company. Over the years they fished, hunted and shared unforgettable times around campfires. He was Tam's introduction to the risk-laden challenges of

Alaska's Southeast, the icy, island-dotted waters between Juneau and the open Pacific.

Herb had recently fallen and broken his hip. The crusty old fisherman lived within walking distance of Tam's house, a couple of turns and a stream crossing away, in a doublewide trailer surrounded by flowers. Herb's petite, spunky wife Erma greeted us at the door. Thee Erma who had sized my boots.

Erma held court with me over tea at the dining room table while Tam and Herb shared shots of bourbon in the living room. Their small home was a welcome reprieve, cozy and bright, smattered with family heirlooms. Erma's stories were a one-woman stand-up, like the tale of her youthful arrival in Juneau from Texas, encountering winds so strong she grabbed a light pole to keep from blowing away. *The squall blew my legs straight out* she laughed.

Feisty Erma: she didn't mince words or miss a chance to stand up for her opinions. I watched cautiously as she and Tam butted heads when he would stop by the table on the way to the kitchen. The outcome was always the same: Tam wouldn't back down; no common ground was sought, no matter the subject, leaving Erma exasperated, her gray-haired curls tighter. *He's always got to be right* she said.

Divine intervention comes in many forms. Ten rainy days from arrival the clouds lightened, I kicked my leg over the side of the Thea G and climbed aboard. We were headed to Taku Harbor, twenty-five nautical miles south through Gastineau Channel. I'd say I was over the top, but I didn't want to jinx myself.

Tam's thirty-five-foot Skookum was rustic romantic. Painted cream and green, the wooden working boat was lovely to the eye. Beauty abruptly gave way to function, however, once one stepped inside. The small, spare galley had a teensy sink and a rusted propane stove. There was no toilet and the noisy engine was a few feet from the sitting area. In short, Thea was akin to backpacking on water. My rudimentary sleeping place was down a step from the steering wheel, into the dark, low-ceilinged V-berth in the bow. I shared the space with food boxes. Teak slept on the floor at my side.

My learning curve was straight up. I did as I was told, not asked, with excitement and anticipation. First up was pulling out of the slip. I hauled up the rubber fenders that hung over the outside and prevented two docked boats from touching. I untied from the pier and nervously leapt aboard. Once out of the harbor I loosened the rope on the rubber raft dinghy following behind the Thea G. We slowly made our way toward open water, past moored cruise ships. Tam increased the speed as we chugged south.

Teak stood perplexed with her tail tucked between her legs, while my transition from land to sea was anything but pretty. Sea legs were slow to show up as I stumbled about. In the first hour I walloped my head against a short doorway, ran a fish hook into my thumb and grabbed a blistering steam pipe for stability. Twice. If I'd had a tail I would have joined Teak.

Seeking solace, I climbed the ladder with camera and binocs and headed for the top deck of the boat. Incompetent klutz was not familiar territory. I needed a private place to make peace with the oceanic mix of awe and awkward. To release my pent-up tears. I peered into the gray world, telling myself things would get better. Then it happened. A golden orb separated the clouds. The day turned hot against my flesh as the Juneau ice fields revealed dramatic, craggy mountains. I tore off my t-shirt and beckoned the sun into every cell.

Thus began my restoration. Chum and sockeye salmon jumped through ocean waves on their journeys to the freshwater streams where they were born. They lifted powerfully from the sea, several consecutive leaps in a row... the females to break up their egg sacks, the males to break up their milky sperm.

Griz dug for clams on distant shores. The striking white heads of Bald Eagles dotted the coastal cliffs; their enchanting cries filled the air. This, my new reality. When I glassed to look at one object two-three-four other stunning scenes appeared in the foreground. Never *just* the salmon; *just* the bears. The depth of wonder was unsurpassed.

I returned to a sullen Tam. The cabin was filled with oily smoke and the engine was gratingly loud. I wondered how he could stand it, especially with hearing aids. My seat (the only one besides the captain's chair) was three feet to the right of Tam's, a narrow chair so high I needed a step stool to climb aboard. He managed a smile as I joined him. My eyes jumped between the endless waters before me and the sonar screen on the dash, a series of graphics that showed the depth of water in large numbers and an ever-changing graph of the sea floor below the boat. Handy gadget. A mechanism to show groundswells, abrupt drop offs, hidden depth charges and other unforeseen dangers. I wanted one. Embedded. Wondered if it might have saved a marriage.

We reached the entrance to hidden Taku Harbor mid-afternoon, whereupon Captain tossed me a bulky rubber suit and put me to work. We removed half-frozen salmon heads from the cooler marked BAIT (don't drop the half & half into this one!) and tossed the gruesome heads into large, netted shrimp pots. Tam attached ropes and flung them at a depth of three hundred feet, twenty feet offshore. *They like steep, deep and rocky* he said. The pots sank into the icy waters in a matter of seconds. So deep, so fast, so utterly alien. I shivered. Tam wasted no time. With mechanical preciseness we entered serene harbor waters and dropped a couple of crab pots to a depth of thirty feet. Floating buoys marked the spot. Shrimp and crab. I was about to see a whole new side to this man.

We returned to the crab pots a few hours later. My job was to lean over the moving boat and snatch the line with a hook at the end of a long pole. Aha! My new MO: hooker at sea. Tam put the engine in neutral, grabbed the line and connected it to a pump-driven pulley in one continuous movement. I operated the gears that reeled in the pot. *Not* so smooth and continuous, to Captain's chagrin.

My attention span was in la-la land. How to concentrate on a touchy gear shift as Marbled Murrelets skimmed the waters and whiskered seal heads bobbed up and down. Scoters and loons were everywhere. A grizzly bear sauntered along the shore. Water poured from the pots as Tam reached inside the cage, grabbed the meaty Dungeness crabs and tossed them into buckets. We wouldn't need that just-in-case steak he'd tossed into the cooler, but we threw it on the grill anyhow. We tied to Taku dock as food and landscape coalesced into unfathomable beauty.

Twilight lingered as Tam guzzled gin and tonics and passed out on his narrow berth, putting to rest my hope for fleshy fun. His snores filled the cabin as I pulled on my Xtra Tuffs, jumped onto the dock and headed for shore with Teak. I rationalized the day had been a major physical and mental workout for the captain. He'd last been here with Liz. The waterproof duds he'd tossed me were hers. Sleep for him and memories of a prophetic dream for me.

Moss-covered poles, remnants of a 1902 salmon cannery, protruded from soggy grass. I passed iron skeletons of ancient equipment and leaning houses with rotten steps. I snapped shots of a blue shipwreck hidden deep in a streambed; made my way through water and muck to where the *Blue Empress* had fallen from grace.

Faded paint placed her from Shelby, Montana. How in the world did she end up here?

I sat in the soft ginger light. Musky griz smell filled the air. Two seals rippled the water. Bald eagles cried, lifted off from high limbs and scraped the water with their talons. These lands had once belonged to the Taku peoples whose name translated as "Geese Flood Upriver Tribe." Taku Inlet's name was attributed to Lieutenant Vasilyev from the Imperial Russian Navy. Years later, in 1840, the Taku's traditional lands became home to the Ft. Durham trading post, part of the Hudson Bay Company. This night, the soggy silhouettes of cannery posts rose like skeletons in the remote bay. Humans came and went, Nature conveyed, but the wild prevailed.

There I was, adrift on the changing tides. Tears welled for no obvious reason. To cleanse? Release? Grief had a far-reaching root system. It might start with the present and drop decades, even lifetimes, into the past. Grief tendrils could wrap their way around any story. Tears were my answer. They transformed grief, kept it from crystallizing into bitter results. What better place to grieve than the ocean, the origin of life. Mother Ocean was a vast homeopathic remedy. Her saltwater welcomed mine.

We downed morning espresso to the sight of spouting whales. Okay, call me coffee snob: I'd packed my Bialetti and dark Italian roast. There's no replacing strong java swirled with creamy half & half. I'd taken my pot on horseback, planes, trains and foot throughout the world.

We steered for the two shrimp pots situated on a steep underwater cliff. I watched with anticipation as the motor and pulley brought the pot closer and closer. The first cage surfaced and was … (drum roll) … empty. The second contained … what!? A dozen empty shrimp shells, a brown bulbous sea cucumber and one satisfied shrimp thief, aka octopus.

Tam pulled the slimy bandit from the cage and tossed him onto the boat floor. Teak was on alert. I watched as the three-foot soft one with three hearts glided effortlessly up and over buckets and ropes with underwater grace. His suction cup legs didn't impede, despite the fact that each cup was capable of lifting thirty pounds. *I'll never kill another one, they're too smart and gentle* said Tam. Some people ate octopus, some used them for bait, but this one would live. With Teak's and my curiosity satisfied, Tam lobbed him into the chilly sea. With one potent eight-armed stroke, he disappeared in a cloud of dark ink.

With Captain Tam at the helm, our next stop was a kelp and krill-filled cove. Thousands of herring bubbled to the surface, attracting clouds of gulls and eagles that skimmed the water for easy takings. Tam fished herring for salmon and halibut bait, part of the chain in the ongoing drama of land and sea. With a bucket of herring secured, we stepped below. Love making, like the landscape that enveloped, was raw and edgy, draped in the gentle rock of Thea G.

I took my topside seat as we chugged toward Juneau. I was ready for solid ground; to leave boat life's state of hyper-alert behind. The watery lands were not for cowards. One misstep could send me overboard. I remembered Tam pointing out flashy new gill netter boats captained by women. It wasn't uncommon for husband-wife sea careers to turn solo when the husband was swept overboard. One wife had steered for hours before she realized he was gone. I wondered if the Sirens were in cahoots with the wives. Divorce humor.

We pulled into Juneau Harbor around 5:00 p.m. I gently put my hand on the Thea G's rail and whispered thanks for a safe return. I stepped over the rail and snapped pictures of Thea for Tam. Then, as if on cue, a light drizzle began to fall as the sky closed down.

We offloaded our supplies and returned to the house, the space more dark than ever. Showers continued for a week. I donned my raincoat twice a day to walk and explored seaside trails. Blueberries, thimbleberries and salmonberries were profuse. Meanwhile Tam's birthday loomed. He said he didn't do presents. That wouldn't do. I emailed a Colorado friend and requested a box of Salted Nut Rolls, his favorite. Hell, if he didn't want them I'd eat them. I had no idea how his birthday, or any other day, would go. It depended on whether or not I engaged his sweet, loving, horny, funny early-day guy, or his short-tempered, gin-inspired, late-day outbursts. I devoured the best of him and Tai-Chi'd myself around the worst, sidestepping head-on collisions, perfecting the art of life with a guy guide.

The rain was ever-constant, unlike the big-droplet downpours of the Lower-48. The leaves did not move on the trees yet I would step outside to downpours. Meanwhile, we gorged. From the freezer came the makings for Dall sheep tacos and moose sausage. Preferred accompaniment: hunting stories. And always, fresh crab salads.

Tam's late July birthday was blue-sky clear as we packed the skiff with shovels, gallon buckets and picnic fixings, intent on reaching Admiralty Island. We pulled out of Auke Bay a little after 7:00 a.m. I'd say dawn, but there was no dawn because there wasn't much delineation between dark and light. No moon to chart the monthly cycle. No sun to follow or get one's directional bearings. Having untethered from job, marriage and my Southwest home of over twenty-five years, this cosmic flotation was an incomprehensible surprise; not to mention unnerving.

Tides dictated this trip. We needed high tide to make it over a shallow approach and into Barlow Cove. We needed low tide to embark on one of Tam's passions: digging for clams. Seas were calm as we left the harbor. This little boat, which resembled a metal row boat, was a rougher, colder ride than the Thea G, but she was much faster and easy to maneuver. I was decked out in rain gear, Teak between my legs. It was another charmed day.

The tide was due to reverse at 10:00 a.m. An hour after departure we anchored six feet off shore. Teak leaped for land and grabbed the nearest stick to play fetch while Tam instructed me to look for give-away slits in the sand; an X would mark the spot of a buried clam the size of a salad plate. That's how big they were. Really?

We walked the beach back and forth but found none. Tam looked like he'd lost his best friend. He was accustomed to getting his way, digging buckets full in a short time. Could it be the red tide? There was a warning not to gather shellfish along the islands, including Juneau, where one woman had eaten clams and died. Tam strode up and down the beach; one hell of a birthday downer. Then, thirty minutes before the tide was to turn the slits split the sand. *Rednecks* he hollered! *Here's another! Shovel on the sea side, a foot down to each clam.* They were six to eight inches across. The biggest clams I'd ever seen. Ye-haw. Dig it!

Tam said hardly anyone knew about the rednecks. I, on the other hand, knew lots about rednecks, but not the clam variety.

The tide turned, marking a dramatic energy shift. In just a few moments the anchored skiff sat differently on the water; holes we'd dug had disappeared and a bucket of clams was surrounded by sea. We gathered the gear, Teak jumped in the boat and we headed for another shore. A two-point buck in velvet and a couple of does grazed near thick pines, their coats a stunning orange rust color.

Forever the multi-tasker, Tam set three crab pots in the cove and headed for a shale-rock shore where we sat, cleaned and shucked the clams. He carefully cut the muscle and extracted the soft, fleshy clam from the shell. I pulled out the picnic basket with chilled Gewürztraminer wine (my favorite), a smoked salmon dip (his favorite), some Cambozola cheese (our favorite), seedy crackers and, voila, Salted Nut Rolls for desert. He smiled that shy smile and took a bite. Idyllic was the word of the day. Tam continued to shuck as Teak and I walked the shore. Miles of untamed harbor to ourselves.

We headed back around 3:00. The winds picked up. The sky darkened. The sea calmed a few miles from shore, allowing a stop onto a small island where we hiked and threw some fetch sticks for Teak. A sweet Winter Wren hopped about a downed tree. Hot pink fireweed grew amidst sharp rock outcroppings; moss hung from feathery hemlock in soft, lovely circles. A Bald Eagle monitored our movement from her perch in a snag. The little island's sentinel lifted off, as a white tail feather separated from her glorious fan. It drifted down … I walked to meet it … I reached … it floated into my hands.

Once home, Tam split the clam meat in half and pounded the fillets flat with a large mallet. Then he breaded and fried. More sweet meat. We joked about the red tide as he took first bite. *If I drop dead, don't eat* he said with a sexy wink. He knew more about the safety of our dinner than he let on, but I still felt I'd cheated death. Then again, I cheated death every time I went out the door in Alaska. Eagle feathers drifted down, down comforters coming down on me.

Down the drain was yet to come.

We decided on a trek with a thousand-foot elevation gain. Slick rock, mud and splendor. I struggled to climb and keep balance as Tam strode gracefully up the mountain, fishing pole in hand. He didn't go anywhere he couldn't fish.

The destination was high-mountain Salmon Reservoir, a snow melt water source for Juneau. There was also a dam built in 1914 that harkened back to a Mayan ruin; plants and moss seemed to seep from deteriorating walls. The handsome, curved structure was the world's first constant angle arch dam; a resident Bald Eagle perched on top. Lemon-yellow monkey flower grew at water's edge.

Eagle watched our every move. I took a seat and journaled while Tam fished for brook trout. A pissed off Kingfisher let loose with a cry and zipped by Tam's head as he reeled in one after another. Tam caught a dozen and cleaned six as mountain goats walked the craggy peaks at snowline. The magic never ceased.

I saw many old plant friends this day, including deep purple monkshood and my favorite petite red and yellow western columbine. Wilson's Warbler hopped among the thickets; Varied and Hermit Thrushes were plentiful. The sun surprised us as we headed down mountain, bursting shafts of light through the sponge-moss forest. Our reward was dinner plates piled with fresh king crab legs ... foot long shells full of white meat ... an ear of corn and those tasty, firm, pink trout. No more need for cod liver oil capsules. Time to replace them with vitamin D, which folks swallowed by the handfuls in the land of scant sun.

We planted ourselves in front of the television after dinner. We never went out to a movie or to hear live music. Ever. He settled into an overstuffed recliner to watch *Lonesome Dove,* a gin and tonic at his side. He motioned for me to join him, which I tried to do, but was never able to get comfortable. I slid back onto the couch, happier with more space. He eventually passed out in his chair, I read awhile and made my way to bed.

We were both early risers. Mornings were generally quiet (no more TV) but now Tam's landline rang with inquiries about his boat. He'd finally listed Thea G for sale, the beginning of his separation from Alaska. I saw the pain in his face, the realization of life transitioning and the end of a dream. There were many calls over the next few weeks as I second guessed whether I should have taken those spiffy photographs he used for the ad. As with all sales, at some point the energies would align and a buyer would show up. I just hoped it didn't happen before the end of September.

Chum (dog) salmon converged throughout Juneau at the entrances to the creeks where they had birthed. Some were lonely pairs, others were bunched by the hundreds, an undulating spectacle of pink and green. The further inland they traveled into fresh water, the more their protective sea water coat wore away. Their organs began to disintegrate. Time was short.

The female wiggled dimples into the shallow gravel and sand among colored stones. She laid thousands of eggs as the male fought off competition and took his place beside her. Poof. He released a cloud of milt to fertilize her eggs. And then, the regal fish that had lifted from the sea in graceful arches, died, filling forests with pungent, dry-heave stink.

I crouched and photographed their muscled upstream struggle, witness to the one of the most poignant displays of biological imperative. Women, too, once died after their reproductive years. A woman's life expectancy in 1900 was fifty years. Modern medicine now kept us vital beyond. While many women were slow to grasp the gift, others saw the opportunity to jump tracks and begin life anew.

Humanity was in new territory. The Creatrix (female creator) archetype was born, snuggled in between Mother and Crone: the perfect time to quest.

I was mesmerized by the salmon's power, their beauty in their call to death. We must keep the rituals intact. Pull the rusty shopping carts from streams that the salmon may return. Give thanks to the eagles and brown bears who lined creek sides to catch the soon-dead bodies as they floated downstream. I stopped snapping and lowered the camera. Whatever road I chose, I would live a good death.

The Food and Drug Administration had recently proposed regulations that would allow genetically modified fish and animals to land on our dinner plates. Genetic engineering already culminated in higher yields and disease resistant crops like corn and cotton. This decision marked the first time modified animals would be cleared for human consumption.

Salmon were first on the agenda, as a Massachusetts company sought approval for a Franken-fish that would reach market size in sixteen to eighteen months instead of the normal three years. A cross between a Pacific Chinook and an Atlantic Salmon, they would produce growth hormones all year long, unlike normal salmon that slowed growth during the colder months. GMO salmon didn't have to be labeled.

GMO foods and plant concerns are countless. Mounting evidence shows that genetically engineered products may disrupt human hormone balance, cause developmental problems in children, interfere with reproductive systems and lead to higher rates of breast, prostate and colon cancer. Younger puberty onset in girls is thought to be a direct outcome of artificial hormonal influx.

And what of the likelihood of forever altering genetic diversity? According to a study from Purdue University, if just sixty transgenic fish escaped into the sea and bred, the original species would be extinct within forty generations. Promises of containment and assurances against escape were profuse. But if the BP Gulf oil catastrophe had taught us anything, it was to not trust promises of those chasing profit. Accidents happen.

What is most troublesome about Franken-fish, however, is how animals are yanked from their evolutionary chain. Species develop within an intricate context of environment, seasonal cycles and surrounding life forms. The earth is a matrix of checks and balances that reinforces the rituals of reproduction.

GMO creations are outside of spiritual reach; a break with the rituals that have evolved to celebrate and give thanks for, say, the salmon that return after years at sea to the fresh water streams where they were hatched. In the midst of their miraculous journey they select a mate. In unbelievable spectacle, thousands of salmon back up at the entrances of their home streams where the fish pair and face rushing downstream waters.

When we eat we digest more than calories. We take in the earth and sea embedded in our foods' life cycles. From the immeasurable festivals, like those of Donny's Tahltan People, to the internationally renowned corn dance on the Tewa Pueblo in Santo Domingo, New Mexico, food source has been rendered sacred; assured through ritual. GMO foods are a vital break from source, catapulting humans even further from our place in the food chain, wreaking physical, environmental and spiritual havoc.

We must know our food. Chew long, swallow gently. Give thanks.

We pointed our bikes up Montana Creek, a narrow trail through dark forest bordered with high mountain glaciers. The sun shone through clouds; the air was clear and sharp. Tam stopped briefly to sink a line. Cast, reel in. Cast, reel in. His mantra. I watched as in a trance, when I suddenly remembered a dream from the previous night. I was doing various, mundane things and Jay was standing in the periphery. He was there, but we had no connection. No regrets, anger or hurt.

Cast, reel in. Cast, reel in.

O lordy, I missed the sun. And what I wouldn't give for a gaze at the rising moon.

My eyes drifted to the blue-ice glacier as Tam continued to cast and reel. My Iowa farm parents had recently celebrated their 60th wedding anniversary. They had lived a novel, packed with habit and fortified with security. I, on the other hand, had lived a series of short stories. Ritual uprooted in nomadic succession.

Herb and Erma had lived a novel too. On our way back to town, Tam received a call that Herb had fallen and Erma needed help. She couldn't lift him. She asked if Tam could take him to the hospital. I sat with Erma as she waited at home for word from the doctors. Our customary cup of tea before us, she said *You must write your book.* I had given her a copy of *Living on the Spine* and was flattered she had read it so quickly. *You are a wonderful writer.* Erma surprised me. She struck me as someone who kept compliments close to the vest. Then out of the blue: *Liz left Tam because he drank too much; he was a bully, he always had to be right. Finish your book* she repeated. Warning or encouragement? Or a truth leaked in the shadow of fear for Herb?

Home again, Tam made chicken-fried venison steak. He said he hadn't hunted deer for several years because of a huge winter die-off a few years back. The deer were forced down to water's edge by deep snows, easy marks for hunters. Tam had asked Fish and Game to cancel the hunting season for that year. It was too easy; a massacre. His plea went unheard.

We made our eager way to the Thea G's slip on the weatherman's promise of more sunny days. I was psyched! – a ten-day trip to Elfin Cove, a fishing village on the Pacific, accessible only by boat or plane. We'd gotten a late start and Captain wasn't pleased. The preparation was excruciating as we hauled weighty carts of supplies and ice down the steep ramps. I prayed the handle wouldn't slip from my fingers; that my feet would keep their traction.

Tam had hung a heavy curtain over the opening where the smoke leaked. The fumes were less toxic but it didn't lessen the grating engine noise. My cabin seat was still an auditory challenge. I envied Tam his deafness. He could turn his hearing aids off. I, on the other hand, stood it only so long before I made my way outside and climbed the ladder to the upper deck, where clouds, whales and mountains merged in orgasmic spectacle. I didn't know my escapes up the ladder angered Tam. I thought he was happy as a clam with his gin and tonic, his sonar and woman-less space. I was soon to learn otherwise.

We threaded our way around Douglas Island, past Point Retreat and south toward Icy Strait. Sea lions slept on large, rocking buoys in the middle of nowhere. Whales spouted and sky-hopped fore and aft. Front and back. Yes, nautical terms were essential, like port and starboard. Yelling left and right could be deadly in the middle of a storm when orders spew forth. Whose left? Yours or mine? Too late.

We anchored close to Barlow Cove where we had clammed on his birthday. Anchorage, a place to anchor. I'd never made that connection. The saltwater breeze melded with silence as we feasted on another crab dinner. All was sublime until Tam's demeanor turned on a dime. He accused me of acting like a *turista* who treated him like a charter boat captain. I deflated; raged from the inside out. *Don't you go there. I'm excited and eager to assist you; I never hesitate. What more do you want?*

Oh god, what to do – trapped at sea with a depressant alcoholic. He couldn't stand my happy demeanor in his life's-all-work scenario. I had the urge to call Erma. She would understand, but what could the wise sage do? No, I would make the best of it. I ducked below and climbed onto my berth in tears, the word killjoy on my lips.

Tam was fun and friendly the next morn, all too happy to point out distant whales and seabirds. Porpoise glided in and out of glassy water. Harbor seals poked their heads from waves to check us out. We fished and dropped crab pots. We lifted anchor and Tam steered us to a sea lion colony on a small island where I photographed the humongous, slug-like males that lounged and barely moved; babes stretched and curled against their mothers. Groups of young ones fished together off shore. And always eagles, their cry, their haunting chirp. As we departed Swanson we passed a small rock island with one tree, a large stick nest and a pair of eagles. They return to their same nest yearly, adding to their nest with fresh sticks. Some nests eventually weighed a ton or two. I wondered how many years it would take for this nest to fell the lone island tree; pondered the price the eagles would pay for their solitary locale.

That night, anchored in a nerve-calming cove, we noted the snazzy names we'd seen on boats – Angoon Trader, Nitty Gritty and The White Raven. Wind Spirit. Mermaid Song. Many a bottle of champagne had christened bows in an effort to right their energy with the sea. We were jogging the memory banks for more names when in floated a luxurious fifty-foot sailboat named Bob. We cracked up. Bob... my new metaphor for no pretense. I would add it to my favorite acronym that women knew well: battery operated boyfriend.

To us Tam toasted, as the man with many ghosts reached out to clink glasses. I clinked back, guarded.

We chugged west toward open sea. We were close to Point Adolphus. I glassed ahead to see several boats and kayaks stopped dead in the water. Tam pushed ahead. He knew why. He maneuvered toward millions of herring that boiled at the surface of the sea, creating a swirling, shiny carpet so thick I could have walked across the waves. And then, as if on cue, a pod of whales appeared, feeding on the fish.

Tails, fins and black gleaming bodies swirled round and round, tightening their circle, producing a wake of bubbles to corral the small herring. In stunning, instinctual strategy, the whales rose in unison to swallow the herring into their gaping mouths. I watched the colossal ones in awe as Tam jigged fifty herring in fifteen minutes, bait for shrimp and crab pots. Jigged: dropped a fishing line with multiple hooks and yanked up manifold fish in a few seconds' time. No bait necessary; the fish were attracted to the shiny hooks. Humpies rose, fishing line sank, man yanked, herring down throats, herring into buckets. My heart stopped somewhere in between bubble feeding whales, a sparkling fish line and the baleen ballet.

Tam revved the engine and powered us on. Someone had to cuz I never would have left. We paused a few miles away where he dropped a line and snagged a halibut. He threw this into the bucket with the Dungeness crab we'd caught the night before.

We weren't far from our destination, Elfin Cove. Just two months earlier my Vibram-soled hiking boots clenched sandstone; now they clung to wet wood as slippery as black ice. Three months ago I had spoken in Taos on the return of the sacred; now I was rendered mute by Alaska's undomesticated world. Four months beyond divorce papers I floated into single life on the Thea G and her raw revelatory basics, right down to the bucket that served as a toilet.

Murrelets bobbed on our foamy wake, appearing and disappearing with aplomb behind watery curtains. Lost in their hypnotic sway, my mind popped with the certainty that I was where I should be, my direction true, without a clue where I would land. Nomad. Dromomaniac. Call me what you may. No thing satisfied as good as freedom felt.

"Conceive a space filled with moving," wrote Gertrude Stein. Until now I had attributed her words to the vast southwest. Now I added watery straits to that list. No fences stopped the natural flow. No wires sliced the sky. A literal life of creature comfort, I would follow the Siren's song. I had the moxie to believe she sang a different tune for Wander Woman.

Teak's bark broke the dawn. I rolled from beneath my sleeping bag and stepped onto the deck. No flashlight required; it was 3:00 a.m. On a shore thirty yards away were four otters, skittering across rock and slipping into the sea like little ghosts. *Good girl* I said into Teak's contented eyes. I was amazed she had smelled them as she slept in the windowless hull. My little Lab. *Best dog in the world.* Her biggest challenge was peeing. The same could be said for me. But Teak couldn't sit on the boat side, hang her butt over and let loose – careful, quick and proud. Nope, she insisted on waiting until the end of the day when we'd anchor, load her into the dinghy and take her to solid ground.

Our sojourn continued toward Elfin Cove. A solitary Humpback breached straight up and fell like a giant tree in an explosive splash. Then he surfaced, lay on his side for minutes on end and slapped his pec on the water. A Humpy's fin is 1/3 his total length; this one was white as snow. Ker-plunk! Ker-plunk! A captivating show of strength.

The meaning of this slap is a mystery. Scientific theories abound, but honestly, I was weary of trying to explain the unexplainable. Ker-plunk. Splash. Let the mystery be. I closed my eyes and stood in the wake of utter power. Imagined my old life coming loose like so many scaly barnacles. Sinking into the sea.

I glassed the water as we neared the open Pacific, looking for floating debris that might damage the underside of the boat. Ah, there: drifting logs in the middle of Icy Strait. Then they moved. Not logs at all, it was a raft of sea otters, floating on their backs! I squealed as we chugged closer, spied a baby on mom's belly. The depth finder portrayed rich kelp beds below the surface. Tam cut the engine and we watched the pure joy of their interplay; constant care and connection, floats and dives. They, so at ease in their isolated, cold water world. I could have watched for hours. Alas, we needed high tide to slip through the narrow channel ahead. The engine ignited with a belch of smoke.

Open ocean came into view as we turned south to Elfin. A trilogy of greetings donned the rock cliffs as we entered the cove. First, a huge nautical red cross WARNING for shallower waters and cliffs. Fifty yards beyond, a bright, stuffed child-sized Mickey Mouse sat in an old wooden chair. Beyond that, protruding starkly from rock was a white cross three feet high. I reckoned that someone, at some time, had missed that first sign. Tam slowed the engine, Teak's cue to jump up and sniff for land.

There were two harbors in the cove. One was on the ocean side where the sea planes docked to bring passengers and mail. A second, larger dock was situated around a rocky hill, nestled into the belly of the town. We chose the small, outer one, in the company of independent, hardtack fishermen. In contrast, the spacious docks of the commercial fishing lodges loomed from the steep shore in front of us.

Fog shrouded us as we tied to the dock. I debarked and took Teak for a stroll. Elfin Cove was a series of buildings built into the cliffside, like a miniature, wooden Machu Picchu. Slippery boardwalks snaked around the hill that overlooked water arteries. Slimy boardwalks, I soon discovered, made slicker by dog shit. I slid right by one gift shop.

There was a post office, a small museum and a fishing supply store. A tiny store was packed with generic trinkets. Pam's Famous Smoke House was closed, but a small grocery store stocked necessities. I was way beyond pedicure-land. There wasn't even a place to buy ice. It was too expensive to freeze.

The only way in or out was by sea or air. Elfin, however, had been discovered by the charter industry. A few modern lodges covered chunks of real estate for the folks who flew in to catch trophy fish. There was a war going on in Elfin Cove, as men who had fished these waters for decades ran up against the moneyed charters. "Charter Fishing is Organized Crime," was a common bumper sticker affixed to boats, in concern that charters would overfish. From where I sat, watching their boats come and go, they also changed the tempo of the community, from easy does it to hubbub; from weather time to linear.

I watched as a charter boat motored into its private dock and six Cabela-dressed fishermen poured out, followed by crewmen with the day's bounty. The catch of the day was larger than I. The halibut was hung by her gills onto the scales, topping two hundred pounds. The man who caught her took his place by the flat brown mother fish as cameras snapped. He looked a little flummoxed, perhaps caught between the heroic catch and a subconscious realization that she carried millions of eggs, the future generations of the species. Photo op complete, he awkwardly stepped away, glanced at her and said *NOW what do I do?* No worry. A crew would clean, fillet, divide her into chunks and put her on ice. The charter lodges had their own ice houses. They'd box her up tight and she'd fly to designated homes.

Fog was soupy-thick as we waited and wished for visibility. There was a rocky area with irregular bottoms and ledges where Tam wanted to fish for rock fish. I'd never heard of them. He claimed them to be the firmest, tastiest white fish. I pulled a Coke from the cooler as clouds lifted enough for us to venture out. It'd been years since I'd drunk a Coke that wasn't accompanied by rum. My body craved sugar in what I guessed was her last ditch effort to balance the salt water and air.

It wasn't long before awe conspired with mist. Humpback whales breached and mixed it up with sea lions. Circling, circling, they rose from the depths, mouths gaping, water and seaweed dripping down their bodies in waterfalls of green. We halted the boat adjacent to a stone island lined in cormorants and gulls. Tam dropped the line and began his rhythmic setting of the hook a few feet above the bottom. Back and forth went his arm, his thumb on the spool, slowly letting out line in his familiar, fluid motion.

Puffins squawked, lifted from the water and shook their wings. Otters bobbed on the waves as boundaries dissolved upon the watery Serengeti. Two hours later, the magic of that rocky shore erupted in every sweet bite. I could even taste the rain. The liquid sun.

The ocean lapped a hypnotic lullaby a few inches from my head as the boat rocked me toward sleep. If I wished a place to birth anew, my narrow v-berth sleeping space in the forepeak of the boat was the perfect delivery room. Dark. One small round hole of daylight. A ceiling so low I couldn't sit up. I had to push hard to roll out of bed, feet first, to hit the floor. What began as a clumsy breach birth a few weeks ago was now smooth, dare I say, sailing.

Teak and I stepped quietly past snoring Tam, into the cloud-shrouded morn. Moored ghost-like, across from the Thea G, was a stunning white fishing boat. Her name filtered through the fog in stark red letters: PAGAN. My imagination went wild. Would I hear drumming in the night; an invocation to Lammas, perhaps? I smiled. There had been several boats I had wanted to board. Invictus, a sweet, small fishing boat had grabbed my imagination. White Raven, a spiffy sailboat with sleek, quiet lines had beckoned me. But this silent arrival topped them all. Alas, I never spied a soul on board, which left me to imagine a haunted galley and smooth-bedded berth; a faceless persona who dreamed within her Siren-sent walls.

Out of ice and clearly in begging mode, we approached the crew of a newly-docked fishing boat who sold us a few bags. One last Teak walk and we pointed Thea inland. Fog gave way to azure sky, titillating waterfalls and horizontal cloud threads over the mountains. In a glory-be reprise, the Humpbacks bubble fed again off Point Adolphus.

We continued east through Icy Strait bound for Hoonah, a Tlingit Indian village with pay showers. Bring it on! My salty hair and skin were desperate. We stopped along the way and dropped shrimp pots onto a rock outcropping called The Kittens. Tam then steered away from shore, cast a line and hooked a shimmery silver salmon within minutes. *Grab that gaff* he barked, as he reeled in the fish with fight. Say what? I'd used the hook on a pole for the pots; seen two sizes on the deck and watched him secure a fish at boatside through the gills, but he'd never called it a gaff. *Where is it?* I yelled. *Next to you by the door! You're just like my dad, always fucking up on purpose.* Oh really? I was in crazy land and two things were clear: he was dealing with ghosts that preceded me and no matter how misplaced his insult, part of me wanted to jump overboard when I couldn't respond competently.

There wasn't time to process. I shook it off as we returned to the pots, gaffed the lines and started the pulley to lift the shrimp pots. Our eyes widened as the pot rose toward the boat. *I don't believe it!* said Jekyll-Hyde.

There were over one hundred fist-sized shrimp. *The most I've ever gotten in one pull!* He looked up at me: *Not a word.* Shrimp hot spots were guarded with a cloak of secrecy, akin to mushrooming sites in the Lower 48. We grabbed the wiggling shrimp and tossed them into five-gallon buckets of salt water. Tam took his place on the back of the boat, smiling wide. He laid a piece of plywood over the cooler and methodically cleaned and filleted the dark orange flesh of the salmon. Tiny silver scales dotted the deck, shimmering like mica in the sun. Or were they tears?

I thanked Goddess every day for the high deck, my sanctuary. Peace. Solace. Sunshine. I usually paid a price when I returned below.

Silent treatment; a put down. It didn't matter. The ladder had become my escape hatch, just as the Murrelets had grown to be my comfort companions. The small chunky birds graced the sea in pairs, floating and diving in unison as the boat neared within a few feet. When separated, their loud peeps pierced the air. The winged wonders lived in western hemlock and Sitka spruce old growth forests, up to forty-five miles inland from shore. They laid one egg in a lichen nest, fed their chick herring and other small fish for forty days. Then, miraculously, the chick fledged and flew alone to the ocean. Here they were, gliding effortlessly upon glassy waters. The perfect little couples, a comforting symbol male/female balance within myself.

We turned south toward Hoonah, the island town located on Chichagof Island. A cruise ship anchored off shore, boating their throngs to land to partake of their private zip line, seaside bar and cafe. Around the bend and out of sight of the ship was the picturesque, quiet harbor. I loved it immediately. Couldn't wait to jump onto the dock, shower, and make my way into town with Teak. The village of Hoonah was about two-thirds Indian, but Tam remembered when all but three people were First Nation.

I entered a fishing supply store to look for postcards. It was 7:00 p.m. They were officially closed but the owner welcomed me inside. Ah, a woman's company! I was like filings to a magnet. She told me of coming to Hoonah from Connecticut with her new husband over thirty years ago. Such a monumental move to this isolated village, reached only by sea or air. We chatted on. She invited us to dinner the next night. Damn, it wouldn't work; we planned to depart the next morning.

We hugged goodbye and I headed back to the boat. As I walked down the street I understood her desire to settle into this quaint place.

Hoonah meant "village by the cliff" in Tlingit. I had the feeling that I could do the same. I thought of those Murrelets flying many miles to sea to dive for sand eels, herring and perch. Sometimes one must travel far for nourishment.

That night I dreamed: A whale watching crew was a cover for terrorists who planned to set off nuclear bombs. I wasn't concerned at first. I was with my daughter Hope but I didn't say anything to her. As the detonation time got closer I panicked. I ordered Hope to run as bombs exploded in the distance. I ran to her and also to collect the evidence from the crew, terrified of getting caught. The explosions were so vivid I awoke shaking. Teak came over and stuck her nose in my face. I reached down to pet her. *It's okay, Teak. I'm okay.*

When we don't pick up on warning signs in real time, dreams embed messages with symbols we can't ignore. I remembered the dream at the beginning of this trip about Tam being married. Now nuclear bombs were going off. My captain was an alcoholic, that wasn't going to change. Tam was a sweet caring man until early afternoon when shame-bombs exploded. I was messy. I was a prima-donna. I was like his father who irritated him on purpose. It was only a matter of time before he compared me to Liz. *You're two peas in a pod* he said.

Two peas in a pod? I asked the next day. I had waited until he was sober. He listened intently and was truly apologetic. We made agreements to prevent future outbursts, retained closeness and headed into the day feeling good. And then, it happened all over again.

I generally stay away from words like "always" and "never" but in this case it was true: there was never progress with an alcoholic. I pulled myself together and reminded myself why I was there. Open sea adventure. To birth a solo life. I added character building to the list. With every passing day, I loved my company more.

We pulled into Thea G's slip, capping another miraculous journey. Fuzzy-headed with exhaustion, exhilaration guided me up the steep ramp to the van. I unleashed Teak at the top, a chance for her to finally romp and pee. I turned to Tam and smiled. *Thank you* I said, with gratitude.

He looked down, looked up, and exploded: *Get that dog on the god damned leash!* The *SNAP!* resonated through my body. I was done. No more fits; no more scolds. We arrived at the house and I beelined for my phone. I made reservations for two weeks hence, one month earlier than planned, on the August 31st ferry to Skagway. Tam took the news stoically. That night he turned off the television, stopped drinking early, dropped into bed and read.

The first labyrinth I had ever walked was at Ghost Ranch in New Mexico. Modeled after the famous labyrinth at Chartres, the stunning circle unfolded upon red rock desert in the shadow of Pedernal, the mountain Georgia O'Keeffe claimed as her own. I had followed its half-mile course in walking meditation to the metaphorical center of the cosmos. I had since walked every labyrinth I came across, from Colorado to Montana to British Columbia. Labyrinths were four thousand years old; they were a bridge to ancient memory as well as present revelation. Beyond Juneau was the Labyrinth of St. Therese. The timing couldn't have been more perfect.

I sat at the circle's edge. Tam's judgments had utterly exhausted me. I took several deep breaths. Ever so slowly the weight of stress released from my shoulders. I took two more breaths. Surrender permeated my cells in preparation for my walk. *I give thanks for the courage to quest* I whispered. A kingfisher called from a nearby spruce, perched near a long string of witches hair lichen waving wildly on the breeze.

I entered with reverence. In my hand was a bright orange flicker feather, a symbol of optimism, a steadying force. Labyrinths were unique for their layering, turning paths. Despite the apparent tangled trail, there was one way in, one way out. No digressions, every step a truth-tell. This labyrinth, framed by the sea, was one of the most beautiful in the world. Eagles cried through the mist. A lithe reddish wren hopped along the shrubby edge, as if to cheer me on.

I stood at the entrance. Door-WAY. It was all so Zen. Within ten steps I was flooded with unexpected memories of my travel to the ruins of Tikal. I had flown there at the completion of my photo documentation of the mothers of the disappeared in Guatemala City. I needed relief and the jungle pyramids beckoned. I climbed hundreds of steps to Mayan temple tops where I communed with a Bat Falcon. I watched as toucans swooped below my temple perch; howler monkeys swung from tree to tree.

I smiled and paused; gazed across the ocean and continued to the center.

The Guatemalan moon had waxed full as I bushwhacked up an earth-and-vine-covered temple, not yet open to the public. I sat silent in milky moonlight, overcome with awe, when the roar of a jaguar serrated the air. I jumped with fright, then calmed with the recognition that the cat was deep in the jungle. But her scream served its purpose. She awakened something deep within. I had to get closer.

The next morning I created a medicine bag: my daughter Hope's love note she'd handed me upon departure from Colorado, a crystal and a tarantula totem. I put the bag around my neck, stuck a sage stick into my pack and departed for the jungle. *Where is the jaguar* I asked the diminutive Mayan guard at the border of Tikal. He pointed down a dirt trail and said *mundo perdido*. The lost world.

There were no groundskeepers sweeping vines in this part of the jungle, but there were guerillas of the human sort. Armed foot soldiers with machine guns crisscrossed the faint trail from time to time. They were shocked to see me; not half as much as I was. I stopped, smiled and said *Hola*. I assumed the best since I was on their side. They, like the army they fought against, had no inclination to mess with Americans. They quickly said *Hola* and trotted on, leaving me to the Mot-mots, Toucans and the unseen creatures of junglescape.

I'd walked an excited hour when I heard a grunt and growl. Jaguar! The sound came from a ravine to my right. I stepped off trail to a small, moss-covered temple and took a seat to collect myself. I made a rudimentary altar, burned sage and listened. My heart raced. I began to sweat. Why was I doing this? No one in the whole wide world knew I was there. I could disappear without a trace. No answers. Didn't matter.

I started down that ravine twice and turned around in fear as I drew closer to the guttural sounds. One more time. I rounded a corner and met her raven eyes. She was standing over a red-meat meal and looked up in surprise. For two seconds we were kin. Then we sprang, in opposite directions. I'd never scaled a hill so fast. I reached the temple, panted my way back to normal, shook and cried.

I paused within the labyrinth walls. Goosebumps covered my arms. The ocean breeze kicked up as I neared the center.

I had wandered in a daze across the grounds of Tikal; stopped before a temple and stared as my body decompressed. A man approached, nodded at the temple and shook his head in admiration. *Temple of the Jaguar* he said. Of course, what else? He introduced himself and offered me his hand. *Hello. I'm Christina.*

I flinched. I'd been Chris for all of my life. Now, from out of the blue with no forethought, I had claimed the moniker of my namesake, Danish Grandmother Christina. Or more to the point, she and the jaguar spirit had claimed me.

I reached the center of the labyrinth and laid my feather offering down. I wished I'd had the courage not to flee that day. In my perfect world I would have sat and watched the holy one. Terror took hold instead, and it probably saved me: one does not interfere with wild meals. If I wanted to meet her now I would go to that jungle altar, sit and wait for her to approach.

I stood at the heart of the labyrinth, the end point where one turns around and begins to unwind the rows of circles walked. In a flicker of breath I placed my hand over my heart. *Christina* I said. I turned and began my exit, confident in my quest.

I finished three loads of laundry and Tam ordered a pizza. He prepared salmon eggs for bait, adding brown sugar and salt and setting them aside at room temperature to cure. Twenty-four hours later they would solidify and he'd cut them into chunks. *Best crab bait there is* he said. We wrapped and froze the silver salmon and rock fish, *to take when you go* he said. The words made me flinch. Go. Yes. The final stage loomed as guy guide and I planned the last passage.

A potter in Mexico once told me if you want to learn Spanish, take a Mexican lover. Well, if you want to make cioppino, board a lover's boat and head out to sea. Our destination was a two-day boat trip away, a cabin on Buck Island where Tam, Herb and friends had gathered to hunt, drink and spin tales for decades. Between Juneau and the cabin were the makings of cioppino. We dropped three crab pots the first night out and lifted six beauties the next morning. Cioppino ingredient one!

The teensy cabin oozed with memories. Outside the screen door was a cross to mark Herb's brother's ashes. A fire pit and rope swings spoke of jubilant times. We walked reverently through the sparse cottage, abandoned long ago as age overtook the hearty men and forced them to surrender their wilderness island retreat. The moment was not lost on Tam, well aware that this would be his final visit in the wake of Thea G's eventual sale and his move south.

We anchored off shore from the cabin for two days, making short trips to rocky outcroppings to fish for elusive halibut, dropping shrimp pots along the way. It was the first time Tam did not reel in what he had intended to catch. Skunked on halibut, we lifted cages of large spotted prawns. Cioppino ingredient two!

C, would you pull their heads off and put them into these Ziploc bags? I knew it would come sooner or later. I couldn't keep eating without participating in the kill. *Demonstrate* I said, watching sheepishly. Tam picked up a shrimp, gave it a little squeeze behind the head and it separated from the body and tail. Okie dokie.

It was easy. Too easy. A twist of my fingers and off with their little whiskered heads. Thus began my game of Sophie's Choice: thank you, shrimp, and a fast twist; bless you, twist; four times for four shrimp. Then I clandestinely tossed the fifth, alive, into the water. My deal with the Spirit.

We returned to our anchorage, grilled some shrimp and watched as two deer fawns played on the beach under their mom's eye. Thousands of salmon leaped nonstop, awaiting a change of tide to travel upstream to spawn. The spectacles never stopped. How many photos can one take? Was that a callous on my index finger?

Spirit and stomach full, I stepped below and plopped exhausted into my berth. The boat rocked gently as Teak and Tam snored. I wrapped my Carole-shawl around me like a life jacket and fell asleep until 3:00 a.m. when I had to pee.

I gingerly made my way to the door. The heavens rained starlight, illuminating my way across the deck. I grabbed the cabin corner for stability and prepared to lift myself onto the side of the boat when I glanced down upon a sea of neon green phosphorescence. Un-friggin' believable. I'd dropped into Pixar. I sat on that boat rail and let loose a pee stream I will never forget as the sea parted in waves of liquid green. I sprang from the rail, leaned over and looked down. This was my life. Daily disclosures of disbelief. As if florescent pee weren't enough, a shooting star glazed across the sky.

When did I realize that the mystical night sky was not a random cloak of twinkle? That predictability reigned in the heavenly statures of Orion's Belt, the Big Dipper, the seven sisters of the Pleiades? Venus the evening star, Venus the harbinger of dawn. When did I learn that the stars and planets were trustworthy maps to seasons and migrations, to the ebb and flow of women's wombs, to psyches in need of direction? How had it changed me to fathom that the earth exhaled into an ebony blanket of twinkling dependability?

No wonder I thrilled at the fiery chaos of a shooting star.

Morning unfolded in a muted sunrise through clouds. I couldn't wait to set foot on shore. A seal swam off starboard. His head rose as he blew out air and sank. I was slow to make coffee, then hunger arrived. Tam searched through cupboards for pancake mix. He found the Krusteaz box and opened it, but nothing poured out. He knocked the box against the floor. Nada. He tore the box to discover flour as hard as brickbats. *Guess it's time to throw it out* he said. I picked up the box and took a look: expiration 1984! I bent over in laughter to keep from peeing my pants. *My grandma must have given it to me* he said as he cracked up. French toast it was.

We were about to climb into the dinghy and row to shore when a griz with two cubs meandered into view, right where we would have landed. They lumbered along water's edge, eating thimbleberries, cubs standing on their hind legs, playing and chasing around a fallen tree. *You don't find bears, they find you* said Tam. I, content to be an observer on my private island named Thea G. The family sauntered on and I stepped below to heat water and wash up – face, pits, crotch and feet. It was a new day. We dropped into the dinghy and paddled to shore.

Those griz, however, had jostled reality. They pushed my body into hyper vigilance amidst scenes worthy of TV's *Wild Kingdom.* Hundreds of Mergansers floated off shore. There were Common Murres and Boreal Chickadees. Hundreds of Dunlins flew aerial acrobatics in a black cloud of wings. Thousands of salmon backed up at the inlet at low tide, and where there were salmon, there were bear.

We played a game of Frisbee with Teak and burned the trash. As if by sleight of hand, the beach became a veritable fountain, water squirting up, giving away the buried hiding places of little neck clams. The beach squished as we walked. We dug fast, a few inches down, dumping clams into a bucket of sea water where they would live until we returned to Juneau. I would change the water every few hours. Cioppino ingredient three!

There was one more island to explore; one more isolated mound of protruding rock and earth so mysterious I felt I was the first to set foot. From shallow shore we entered thick forest and undergrowth. Berries and butterflies were profuse. Old growth cedar and hemlock towered above the island sanctuary. We traipsed along a game trail, about a mile in, when Tam turned and said *You go first.* I looked at him askance and took the lead, well aware I had no bear spray.

I rounded a bend. What stood before me was beyond belief – a Sitka spruce branched and curved like a gargantuan, petrified octopus. Countless limbs curved straight up, sky high, others dipped to the ground. Tam's promise of months ago, to show me his favorite tree, was fulfilled. He knew this tree from prior hunting trips; he referred to it as She. I approached with reverence as I followed Her chaos of giant limbs. Some were heavy with moss and thriving communities of ferns. I mounted a limb and scooted up one of the many trunks.

I leaned forward, lay my head down and rested against Her bark. Eyes closed, my memories returned to the ponderosa pine that had instigated my back roads odyssey so many years ago. I would not be here if not for Grandmother Tree tucked in the Sangre de Cristos' steep flanks. I had hiked through snow and sunshine to Her old-growth base to sit and ponder my life. Now it seemed as if the two old ones converged as I remembered Her words. *Flowers do not question the unfurling of their blossoms. Baby birds do not wonder when their shell will break open and they will emerge. Trust the unfolding* She'd said. *Spirit will put you where you need to be; soul takes you where she needs to go.* She demanded the ultimate practice in faith before She ordered me to *Grow your hair long and get going.*

Well, if she were Grandmother, this barked-being was Great-Great-Granny. It seemed as though my quest would be anchored by Sages of the Forest, pointing me down, Persephone-like, to timeless roots. Toward what end, I did not know.

We stayed with Her for an hour, returned to the dinghy and rowed to Thea. That eve we held one another in the waning light.

Thanks for an unbelievable day I said. *You're a good man, Tam.*

He backed away as if I'd stabbed him.

Don't say that. Every ex called me a good man before she walked out the door.

My stomach twisted as we pulled away from Buck Island on a picture-perfect morn. Southeast's magic journey was coming to an end. We would spend the final night where our boat days had begun, in Taku Harbor. I gazed back to the island growing smaller and smaller; our wake disappearing against the shore.

Two hours later we approached Point Hugh. The weather front that prompted our hurried exit had caught us. The wind roared; waves crashed against protruding rocks. Tam slowed and circled back, calculating for tides and wind. He finally cut the engine close-in. He knew how much time we had before we'd drift dangerously into rock. He prepared a line for me. A fine line, I might add. Between the thrill of it all and making a mistake; becoming ammunition for his next happy hour.

My first catch was a bottom-dwelling sculpin. I reeled him in, Tam detached him from the hook with pliers and tossed him back to sea. My bobber tugged again. Sank right out of sight. What was THIS? I was about to meet my first halibut. Not one of those human-sized mothers from the likes of Elfin Cove. This beauty was about a yard long. The best size, said Tam, for flavor. I was over the top. Cioppino ingredient four! Tam snapped a picture and fired up the engines. He'd accomplished what he'd stopped for, the gift of one last fishing thrill.

Captain put me at the helm and lay down for a nap as I steered toward Taku. Winds increased as waves crashed against the boat. Visibility worsened as I looked through a veil of thick mist. Swells were four feet and growing on the open sea. "Safe harbor" was more than just a saying. I was anxious. Our reversed course rendered landmarks unfamiliar. I pointed the boat toward an inlet but the closer I got the more it felt wrong. Blessed be intuition. I believed it to be Tracy Arm, a glacier-speckled, potentially dangerous inlet and a place I would have loved to go, some other day.

I woke Tam and asked for help. He went off on me. *You should know where to turn.* He wouldn't stop yelling as he took the helm, berating me for an hour ... an hour! – until he got to his underlining complaint: *You do what you want. You defy authority!*

Stop it! I wasn't defying authority. I was unsure. I asked. He took out his hearing aids and turned away. Damn bully boatman ... defying? Calm down, Christina. Breathe.

I was not alone in my impasse at sea. Hemingway's granddaughter and her husband had similar experiences. Réanne's book subtitle said it all: *One Man's Dream, One Woman's Nightmare*, as she recounted their failed attempt to sail around Cape Horn. She endured weeks of insults and arguments: "You don't understand a goddam thing!" her husband had yelled, "I explained that already ... you can't conceptualize, can you? But at least you should be able to listen." Her response was to give him a dirty look, withhold sex, and hop on the pilot berth with her journal, furious. It was all too familiar.

I slipped past Tam and into my darkened berth, moved my vest to make a pillow and behold! - my truck keys fell out. Keys I didn't know I had. My future. Hook up Perla and start the engine. Furthermore, I smiled, defying authority was a compliment.

Tam's outburst sucked. On this, our final night at sea, we were back where our Southeast ventures had started. Taku's refuge could have been so very special. Moby Dick meets Wander Woman, a no-holds-barred kinda thing. But we didn't come close. He harangued me all the way into the harbor, drank himself into a stupor and passed out. Good show, Captain.

Teak and I hopped ashore, visited with a thirty-something couple who floated in on a gorgeous catamaran with their five-year-old spirited daughter. I bid farewell to the phantom-like cannery ruins before planting myself on the top deck, pointed toward sunset. There were no whales in sight. Cioppino secured, I'd earned my water wings.

The open sea ripped Thea with boat-smacking swells as we turned north to Juneau. I was terrified, clenching my way across the bucking-bronco deck and into the cabin. I sat next to Tam as he recounted life-threatening storms much worse than this. I couldn't erase the image of Réanne Hemingway and her husband pitchpoling off Cape Horn. No, thank you very much.

We made our way to the slip in silence. My nerves were jangled. My body ached as tears of relief ran down my face. The drive to his house was thankfully silent. We showered and fell into bed, totally spent. No eye contact, no goodnight. I dreamed I looked out the window and saw Pooka. She was faded and scraggly. I yelled her name and ran to pick her up. *Pooka is here!* I said. She'd found me.

Tam snored on as I crawled out of bed the next morning. I'd reached my emotional limits. I couldn't take another verbal attack and I wondered if Pooka was okay. I emailed Jay to ask but he didn't respond.

I donned my rain jacket and set out for Mendenhall Glacier, a spellbinding swath of glacial white that oozed from the renowned Juneau Icefield. I needed nature, and I needed her man-less. I smiled as I passed a woman tourist on the trail whose t-shirt proclaimed: "Alaska Men: The Odds are Good, but the Goods are Odd."

I continued up the paved trail toward the glacier. The air cooled as the breeze wafted over blue-green ice. I came upon an interpretive trail speaker on a post with a red painted question mark. My imagination had a heyday as I pressed the button: *Good morning, Christina, so you wonder where you are? You say you miss classical music, bright colors and joy? 'Tis time to get outta Dodge.* I walked closer to the glacier and pressed the button on the next box: *It takes courage to turn out as you really are.* Hey, you stole that from e.e. cummings. *Don't change the subject.*

It snowed year round on the Icefield, a one-hundred-mile long, fifty-mile wide swath of frozen peaks that separated Juneau from the rest of the world. It rendered the narrow city, for all practical and spiritual purposes, an island. The Juneau Icefield was over twice the size of Rhode Island.

I'd witnessed extraordinary peaks and glacier calves as Tam and I traveled the straights and coves of Southeast. This glacier up close, however, was authentic power. It took twelve inches of snow to make one inch of ice that flowed slowly and powerfully downhill, six inches a day, into the glacial blue lake smattered with icebergs. There were thirty-eight major glaciers in the Juneau Icefield. Ninety-nine percent of the Juneau Icefield glaciers were in retreat and calving faster with climate change. The Mendenhall glacier retreated, on average, sixty feet a year. The last ten years it had retreated three hundred feet a year. The captivating glacial lake before me had melted one month earlier than normal this year. It would not be long before it was a major hike to reach the glacier's edge.

I spied a black bear with three cubs streamside. Mom was giving catch-salmon lessons. She caught a large sockeye and took it to shore. The triplets wrestled, played and ate, and when it was over mom headed downstream at a trot, silently directing the cubs straight up a tree to sleep for the night. Well, two of the three. The smallest babe, left behind on the bank with a salmon skeleton, cried WAHHHH.

Mom returned and walked him to the base of the tree. Up they went, endearing as could be.

I packed in the final daylight hours, preparing La Perla for travel mode. I sat inside my little nest, stealing a few more moments of solitude. Ravens walked around on the rooftop ... clop clup clomp ... they sounded like ebony horses. I would miss them. With computer, printer, books and journals stowed, I returned down the hill to the house, hoping Tam's mood would be bright.

He was busy in the kitchen, double-wrapping packages of crab meat we'd picked and dressed. Before placing them in his freezer to harden overnight, he took a black marker and wrote on each one. Deer cock. Caribou cock. Moose cock. Sheep cock. Muskox cock.

What are you doing? I laughed.

It's for the nosey Canadian border folks when they look in your freezer.

Not to worry I said *I have good border karma.*

The goods were odd all right.

Tam and I collaborated on the cioppino. There was crab from our first day and the little neck clams from the second. There were shrimp and prawns, and on the seventh day there was halibut – the one I caught! Tam added candlelight and a beautiful pink Sitka rose to the center of the table. A fine, butterscotch Chardonnay topped off our final dinner.

We picked crab meat from the shells that floated in scrumptious broth with halibut, shrimp and clams. We sopped broth with garlic bread as we oohed and aahed our way through the cioppino of a lifetime. He said he'd gotten a call on the Thea G and he was going to show her in a couple of days. Meanwhile, he had arranged to dry dock her for the winter. Pull her out of the water to protect her from winter's ravages. *Be nice if I could sell her first* he said.

Do you mean that? I asked. *No* he said.

Tam refilled the wine glasses. I picked up the cork and wrote my name. He followed suit and wrote his. Yes, there was love here. We'd shared moments that defied naming, in places beyond description. We took one another's hands.

You n' me, we're like Venus and Mars he said, as if male/female communication habits could explain away the pain. I know he was trying to reach me. I looked at him through tears but didn't say a word. I wasn't about to spoil a meal made in heaven. No fight on our final night. And besides, Venus and Mars had little to do with it.

The alarm went off at 3:00. Tam followed Teak, me and Perla in his white van as we made our way to the Auke Bay Ferry Terminal. I wore four shades of gray and a red kerchief. *You've got to love gray to stay* I'd once said.

I was not good at goodbyes; I inevitably cried and choked on words before surrendering to silence and a hug. This morning was no exception as we stood by Blue and waited for me to board.

I wish we would have met sooner, when we were younger. He looked from me into the distance as his voice turned inward. *But no, I would have been just another one of your short stories.*

Vehicle engines revved in the front of the line, signal for me to jump into the truck. A long kiss goodbye – ah, they were sweet – finest ever. I hopped behind the wheel. Tam reached inside, petted Teak goodbye and took a step back. *Have fun* he said, his final words. The irony smacked me broadside. Fun? This, from the King of Killjoy. I wanted to punch him. *Fun is my forté* I said. I turned the key, blew him a kiss and drove into the hollow bowels of the Colombia; no glance into the rear view mirror. He could have ridden to Skagway with me for free. He could have come aboard for thirty minutes. He could have …

Stop it, Christina.

My mind flashed back to Arizona and the first time I saw him. He had parked his mountain bike and walked down to the dock where I was throwing fetch balls into the water for Teak. We talked a bit. He had the cutest, little boy smile and sexy body. I knew within a few days that he liked his gin. But we make our deals, ever hope-full for a change of course on turbulent seas.

The ferry guys were experts at directing tires and packing vehicles like so many sardines in a can. It's a good thing because I was an emotional mess. Dogs weren't allowed on deck. I played the *best dog in the world* card, left her in the backseat and began the climb to the upper decks of the Colombia. I entered a child's play corner, did my stretch routine and walked around the ship in a daze. Decided I wouldn't eat breakfast on board when I saw the chef eating from the vending machine.

The upper deck of the ship was open. Those who eschewed the high price of a berth set up tents; many slept on pads and sleeping bags. I was the only person who stirred in the early morning hours as my mind struggled to keep my emotions at bay.

All ferries in the Alaskan system were named for glaciers. The Colombia's namesake was in the Juneau Ice field in Prince William Sound. I stood and watched the changing shades of gray. Boats crawled along the distant shore … trawlers, purse seiners and gill netters and the fishermen and women who staked their lives on the next big catch. I gazed toward shore, remembering Tam's lesson of how to tell if you're drifting. Line up an object in the foreground with an object in the background. Wait to see if the points separate. If they drift apart. *Catch my drift*? he'd said as he kissed me.

No, I was not drifting. I'd journeyed three thousand resolute miles to Juneau, from paint-by-numbers sex to Jackson Pollack florescent brushstrokes. From arid, Wild West wilderness to a wet Serengeti. From a hypothetical "us" to an indubitable "me." I was bound for nomad's land.

Now, if that eagle would please release my heart from her talons.

Alaska Island Sitka Spruce

Part Two

Rumble

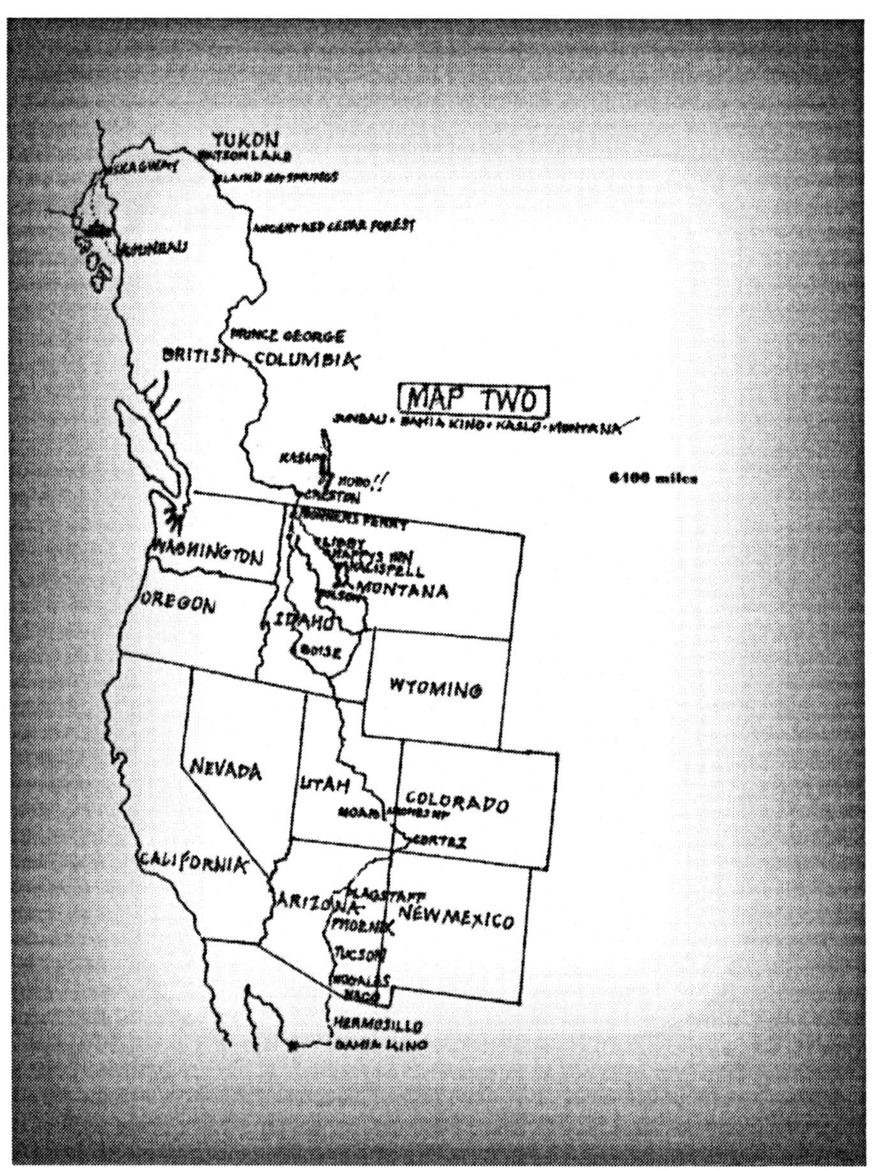

YUKON
PRINCE GEORGE
BRITISH COLUMBIA
MAP TWO
KASLO
CRESTON
BONNERS FERRY
KALISPELL
WASHINGTON
OREGON
IDAHO
MONTANA
BOISE
WYOMING
NEVADA
UTAH
COLORADO
MOAB
CORTEZ
CALIFORNIA
ARIZONA
FLAGSTAFF
NEW MEXICO
PHOENIX
TUCSON
NOGALES
HERMOSILLO
BAHIA KINO

Six hours by ferry to earth and asphalt. If limbo had a color, it would be gray. I slipped in a Mozart cd and drove uphill out of Skagway. I arrived at the Canadian border stop, south of Whitehorse, mid-afternoon. The Customs folks were stiff, in no mood to be cajoled. Perhaps they saw the incongruity between my tears and smile. Something set them off because they chose me for a random-they-said search. I was ordered to take Teak and get out of the truck. Stand in a parking lot twenty yards away. A woman officer searched Perla while a man checked Blue. Like a posse pursuing someone to hang, they searched every article of my life. It was the last thing I needed. There was a crash from inside the trailer; I strode up to the door. *What are you looking for?* I was livid. *Ma'am, step back. You can't be this close.*

Perla's bloodhound finally handed me my passport and said I was free to go. No apology for the hour delay. No accounting for the inconvenience. I took my passport, said their treatment was insulting, loaded up Teak and drove away. I soon pulled off the highway and followed a gravel road to a boondock spot. I stepped outside into a mixed conifer forest; an explosion of purple fireweed, red groundcover, vivid yellow aspen and quiet-oh-gawd peace.

Then I opened Perla's door to disarray. There was a broken ice cube tray on the floor, ice cubes melted in the sink and half-open drawers. *What the … ?* And then I remembered the crash. I guessed the border-gal had opened the freezer and dropped the ice cube tray when she saw Tam's frozen crab-cock surprise. There *was* justice.

I picked wildflowers as Teak and I walked a dirt road. Gone were the piercing eagle cries, murrelet peeps and raven chatter. I sat on a fallen log and began to drum. Let the healing begin. I had drummed for decades, various times with Indian mentors. A drumbeat, they taught, was profoundly healing, the same vibration as the earth.

I didn't understand it at the time. Vibration? What I did not comprehend, however, I trusted. I'm indubitably drawn to things I don't get. The answer was found in quantum physics. Everything vibrates and those vibrations can be measured. A human's normal range is 62-82 MhZ. A negative emotional state drops it by 10-12; a positive state increases it by the same. My guess: an angry drunk went negative. So to speak.

Bring on the drum, the sound that called me home. My arms twitched as tension released. Tears welled and fell. I had driven beyond mad and mean, drink and sink. I was solo on the road again. Or was it soul-o?

I heaved a sigh. This. Was. Huge. Like the jaguar initiation in Tikal, I garnered the courage to quest, unsure of the outcome. I didn't know what I sought. With intuition as my guide, I would live the *quest*ion. Perla would shelter me across wildscapes as I drove the white lines between elation and fear. I would accelerate and brake when I pleased. There would be no wrong choice at a crossroad. I, woman nomad ... womad.

I pulled out *Milepost* and eyed Liard Hot Springs. Perfect. I slept deep and long.

I arrived at Liard in the rain, found a lovely forested space, parked and hooked up. I pulled on the awning and it wouldn't move. Tam had tied it to the supports long ago in Arizona. It now provided a poignant ritual: I took a skinning knife and cut the ties.

Liard's pools permeated my flesh as thunder shook the sky. I rose early to sneak in topless, let the girls float free, as Boreal Chickadee, Swainson's Thrush, Yellow Warbler and Rufous-crowned Sparrow sang songs of morn. One, two, three soaks a day, ten-hour sleeps at night. I regaled a return to simple life, popping corn for dinner with a side of provolone cheese. I hiked in search of the big guys – moose and bear – and saw instead a mellow covey of Spruce Grouse, spread across the mossy earth. Easy marks for hunters, they are known for not bolting; they stay close and are sociable. Praise be, their soft-friend energy.

The plum-colored candle burned down. I was deep into Paco Taibo's *Leonardo's Bicycle* with a glass of Dubonnet as night crept in. Tomorrow I would pack and head down another road.

I hadn't gotten far when a line of rare woodland caribou threaded their way down a rocky slope, crossed the highway and continued down the mountain. I pulled over to witness mothers and yearlings, an astonishing sight. British Colombia's caribou numbers were dropping, prompting dire predictions of extinction. Although wolves were an easy target for their decline, studies confirmed that the number one culprit was industrial development: logging, oil and gas drilling, pipeline and road construction fractured caribou habitat. Caribou were not a primary target of wolves, but the wolves' sanctioned slaughter was easier than slowing the momentum of extractive industries. A theme to be repeated throughout my journey.

I boondocked on a high ridge overlooking a serpentine river named Peace. Teak lazed on her dog bed as I lounged at the confluence of journal scribbles and aromatic espresso. The phone rang a dozen sips in. The screen read Tam. I tentatively picked up. His voice cracked as he forced the words: *Herb died.* Oh geez. *I'm so sorry, Tam.* Our exchange was civil and soft. One might say it held promise.

I phoned Erma, told her I loved her; she was predictably stoic. Decades of Alaska life had roughened her edges. She wasn't with

Herb when he died. He had been transferred to a hospital out of reach. There's got to be a better way to do death.

Hope called later that day. A catch-up how are 'ya that took a turn when she said she'd seen Jay with a prominent woman artist at a dinner party. *She must have money. Meow.* We laughed. The news I'd initially taken lightly eventually hit like a bomb. *I hope you told her that he only apologized once in fifteen years* I said to an imaginary Hope. *And furthermore ... Nope. Don't go there, Christina.* Later that day I bought a black and red mug from a gift store in Chetwynd. My favorite colors since a 1980s sojourn to Nicaragua. The colors of revolution and not coincidentally, independence.

I passed the turnoff, but there was no second guessing. In a rare reversal, I took British Columbia up on its invitation to walk in an ancient forest. *How 'bout it, Best Dog in the World? It's your birthday.* She looked excitedly out the window as we headed up a steep gravel road to a rudimentary parking lot. I donned my raincoat and we were on our way. We had the place to ourselves on the Labor Day break.

Within moments we stood in the striking stillness of western red cedars one to two thousand years old. It was hard to fathom, to think that they sprouted before Copernicus declared the sun did not revolve around earth. Western red cedar, "arborvitae," Tree of Life. When I looked skyward through the canopy, the towering branches framed a round portal to the cosmos. *Sacred circles.*

Gold dust lichen covered the stately trunks. Lichen's fairytale veil didn't begin to grow until the trees were two hundred fifty years old. Here, no tree grew without it. I approached the largest and oldest in this arboreal temple; two thousand years old, sixteen feet in diameter. I kissed her smooth trunk. Gave thanks for our misty meeting.

This forest home was threatened. Just as the warming earth melted Alaska's glaciers and turned seas acidic, the rainforest interior wetbelt shifted. Undisturbed for centuries, like some hidden tribe in Borneo, the consequences of modern consumptive life had found her. There would be no future forests like this.

I returned to Blue, removed my coat and rubber boots, and realized one silver and amber earring was gone. I panicked. I walked the loop trail again to no avail as I recalled the Southwest turquoise-blue day I had spied the sterling silver beauties for sale on a table at Taos Pueblo. It was the San Geronimo Day autumn pole climb and I wanted something special to commemorate a favorite Pueblo ritual. Now, my sunshine amber, ancient as the trees, ceased to dangle from my lobes.

What energy did the Koshare clowns set in motion that day? Amber was born from the resin of cedar. In a sense it had returned home. I pinned a note to a bulletin board in the parking lot with contact information in case the earring was found but I knew it was gone. I'd long had an accurate intuition about lost things. Lost to me, found for the amber. I smiled at the irony and realized the greater significance: ancient trees continued to confer a journey not yet deciphered. Gathering force.

The further south I traveled the more the wild succumbed to towns and landscaped lawns, a transition I resisted. I almost turned back to the Yukon. Instead I found a winding forest road. A dark roadside camp and a ferry ride later, I headed up the lane to meet Carole's jumping bean hello. It's something we've done forever – wrap our arms around one another, hug and lift off the ground at the same time. Sisters.

Chris and Carole's thirteen acres lay vertically on a steep mountain overlooking the one-hundred-mile-long Kootenay Lake. The rugged peaks of the Purcell Wilderness rose across the lake, yet, here was farmville. A half dozen sheep and three turkeys roamed the hillside, lovingly fattened for slaughter. A dozen varieties of hens laid fresh eggs daily. The meat birds (fast-growing chickens) were already butchered and frozen for the winter.

A fresh bouquet of pink cosmos, black-eyed daisies and scarlet begonias graced the table. The counter overflowed with late season bounty: sweet tomatoes, broccoli, eggplant, onions and garlic. *This is savory. Sweeter than the average cabbage* said Carole. It was.

I'd landed in the epicenter of domesticity, overwhelmed by freshness and Carole and Chris's commitment to land, organic garden and the Kaslo community that embraced them. I was relieved to be parked. There was work to do: writing, marketing photographs, organizing reams of notes. It was sweet to awaken into the roominess of unpacked Perla.

Submersed in quiet moments, however, I missed my slippery solitude. The gaze across the sea. A distant whale breach. The steep descent down the ramp at low tide to Thea G. Memories brought longing as the magnitude of Southeast overtook me: the feel of Swan Island, where salmon ejected from the water like popping corn, their instinctual wait for a turn of the tide to make their way home. That night I dreamed of Thea G, awakened and thought I was in my berth. I still had much to unstow.

I stalled at Carole's bookshelf and pulled John Valliant's *Golden Spruce.* Serendipity: I'd never heard of it. According to Valliant, millions of otter flourished in the kelp beds from Alaska to Baja California in 1730. One century later they were all but gone. Beaver, fox and ermine trade opened the West, but it was the sea otter that stimulated the greedy gold rush on the seas for their unparalleled soft coat with up to a million hairs per square inch. Imagine. A million.

I read on, re-living my otter-time on Icy Strait. Sea otters rarely went ashore. They ate, slept and held hands for hours while floating on their backs. They used flat stones to break open shellfish. Stored the stones in skin flaps. Once as "plentiful as blackberries," their home waters were the fog-laden North Pacific. When I'd watched them stroke their dense coats in the chilled waters, I didn't know they were creating air bubbles of heat. Remarkable beings.

Carole and I chose the equinox for our outing. I drove Blue forty miles up a narrow, ledge-hanging 4WD road. Carole had only been to Meadow Mountain once; we took our time, choosing forks in the road with care. *We're almost there* became Carole's mantra. A mantra for my life, I mused. I'm almost there but of course I wasn't. I was right here. We climbed to breathtaking views of lakes ringed by streams of clouds; finally broke through to a glorious 360-degree view of Alp-inspired peaks – and the season's first snow.

We jumped from Blue and stretched into crystal-clear air. Nothing coulda wiped the grins from our faces as we walked along pothole lakes and clumps of tight twisted pine toward larch that glowed like golden torches. We returned to the truck and scraped a layer of heavy snow from a lone, weather-hewn picnic table. The table dried fast under the high-altitude sun. We spread a tablecloth over the wood and unpacked fresh-picked pears, brie, crackers, and crab from Alaska waters. A sweet, light Moscato topped off our communion. Bliss, as we jettisoned our fleece tops, picked up our hide-stretched drums and began a beat.

It had been twenty years. Carole and I had once drummed regularly for workshops we facilitated in Boulder. Now there we were, on top of the world, setting a drumbeat. One of us held steady while the other riffed and vice versa. Intensity and speed rose and fell. Ultimately we fell back into a shared beat; softened and stopped as if someone had lifted our leather-covered beaters simultaneously.

Equinox is an edgy window between light and darkness. One would think on this day of equal day and night that balance would reign, but energetic channels zipped about. Especially with the almost-full moon. Carole spread her Tarot cards upon the table.

Tarot was Carole's forte. I'd never owned a deck but loved the shuffle and spread. I cut the deck; Carole flipped over eleven cards and explained their significance. The problematic ones caught my attention. It was hard to ignore a block wall in the mental realm. Perseverance was a necessity. Another card indicated familial karmic knots soon to be severed. Intriguing but not surprising given the distance between Mom and me since Dad had died. Overall, the cards reflected the wild that nurtured me and a universe that supported my quest. The reading validated my present movement, right down to the edgy reference to karmic knots. Knots set to unravel with volcanic force.

The morning sun drenched our breakfast girl talk as chickens suddenly scattered; the netting over their coop sprang like a spider web that had seized a big bug. I grabbed the binocs. It took a few seconds to realize a bird was ensnarled. We ran for the coop. It was a minute Saw-whet Owl, her wings and talons tangled in string.

Broken wing? Sliced neck? I pulled on leather gloves, stood on a cinder block and held the little one firm as Carole cut. The owl stared with huge, golden eyes. She did not struggle; her only sound was an occasional nervous click. Four precise cuts and the feathered one fell into my hands. I pulled her to my chest and carried her to a nearby log.

Northern Saw-whet Owls are around eight inches tall. They live in abandoned tree cavities, especially pine, aspen, fir, spruce and larch. The varied forest that surrounded Carole and Chris's land was Saw-whet heaven. And so was the cleared pasture space, providing a constant diet of insects, voles and mice for the feathered one. She was probably after a mouse chewing on the broadcast chicken feed. Easy pickings.

The Saw-whet stilled against my heart. Ten precious minutes had passed when I held out my hand and her razor sharp talons clasped my gloved finger. So far so good. She didn't appear to be injured, but could she fly? She perched awhile longer before spreading her soft wings. Eighteen inches of feathers spread horizontally across the air but she did not fly. The nocturnal owls' evolutionary path had selected for those that held still in the presence of predators. Nature had cloaked them in camouflage. They were one of the most trusting beings on Earth. She continued to clasp my finger and perch. Several minutes later she turned her golden eyes to mine and cocked her head. *You're welcome* I said. She lifted effortlessly and rested on a nearby spruce branch. An hour later the brown-feathered marvel was gone.

I needed that surprise to balance growing anxiety. I worried about securing income and writing my next book. I missed Pooka. Jay and Tam showed up in the same dream, as my subconscious worked to integrate the past few months. The owl's appearance propelled me out of the fret zone. Wild encounters do that. They shake up priorities and shrivel the mundane.

Shortly thereafter I scribbled *Drive Me Wild,* the title of my next book.

It was fifty miles up Kootenay Lake to the Monica Meadows trailhead. We'd attempted this hike three years before and were stopped by a landslide. The fates were with us this day as we crept up the crotch of Meadow Creek Basin. The raging creek, strewn with house-sized boulders, made me wonder how the lazy streams of Colorado justified the label river. The Purcell Wilderness, home to Loki and Jumbo Peaks, was another scale of wild.

The hike was a sweaty, steep-step romp. Huckleberry bushes, deep red and gold with autumn, lined the damp path. Snow-laden peaks and receding glaciers framed our views. It took a couple of hours for the trail to gentle. We caught our breath, followed around the mountain curve and dropped into a basin of rare alpine larch. It was like coming across a hidden village I'd longed to see, but didn't know until now.

The alpine larch grew in inhospitable places at tree line in the Canadian Rockies. They were stunted and wind-hewn compared to the towering, heavily-logged family to the south in Montana. They clung to rocky cliffs so precarious and natural it was hard to tell which came first, the tree or the precipice. And in a fit of twisted magic, they shed their needles at autumn's call. *It's like walking into caramel* whispered Carole, as a quiet breeze loosed a soft golden shower upon our skin.

We rested by a pool of reflective water, ate a meager lunch of nuts, cheese and pears, and soaked up the sun. We'd forgotten our usual celebratory treats – no flask of port, no dark chocolate. We took turns posing and snapping photos that would never make it to Facebook, giggling our way to silence. The high mountain mood was exhilarating as we traversed up rocky cliffs. We climbed to the first of three old-growth larch that stood like sentinels on the rocky slope. We said hello, touched her thick trunk and hiked on to the second, a fire-scarred ancient.

The afternoon sun waned as Carole and I took a seat beneath the outstretched branches of the third. We needed to start down, yet couldn't move. Held mysteriously in place, we sat silent. Tears eked from my eyes. Teak gave me a comfort nudge as Carole, too, began to weep. Intense sadness rolled over us as we shared: Why were we on this planet now? How would we possibly maneuver through the mass extinction in progress? What would become of our Mother Planet? Our children and grandchildren? The wild? When did the revolutionary-hope-full-irreverent 1960s take a turn for the dark?

One joyous moment we were at the pond, the next moment, on the mountainside in despair. Joy and despair, yin and yang, two sides of one emotion. Our steps had brought us to the Old Ones to release and cleanse. To root our lives in love and carry on. I stopped on a curve to photograph sundown light on a remote peak. Light and shadow. Everyone carries grief. Nature ensures it does not petrify into pain that seals the soul from awe.

Twenty-four hours before my Kaslo departure I discovered damp walls in La Perla's closet. A climb to the roof revealed a dozen small tears. How the heck? Was it those Alaska Ravens marauding around? Neighbors Ken and Robert showed up the next morn with sealant, caulk and hairdryers. My angels. An early birthday present. That night Robert "collected" me (Canadian-speak) for a farewell dinner at the Kaslo Pub. We talked RVs – it was his dream to trade his life of house and yardwork for months of travel. Our evening together, birthday gift two.

Gift number three was the piece of homemade apple pie Chris slipped me on my way down the road. Number four came the next day: a friendly female reception at the US border. She took my limes with a smile and surprised me with a sudden question about Iowa, my birth state.

Two days from Big Sixty, I slipped down Idaho asphalt, landing in hunting camps ringed with turning leaves and frosty mountain meadows. Cascade Lake – just me, mystic White Pelicans, Goldeneyes, Grebes and Sapsuckers for a shoulder-season $7/night. It didn't take a birthday to accept white pelicano's delicate wing flap over the mirrored lake. Me, wrapped snugly in the present.

A seductive hot spring later I landed in Boise at Johanna's. I'd loved her from the first time we met, at the end of a dead-end road on Lake Havasu. I'd pulled into a campsite and looked down upon her backside as she petted her Labrador Jack. She looked up, laughed and proclaimed I'd already met the best part of her.

Johanna had traveled and trekked the world outback, oft times with one of her child-daughters. Now seventy, she lived near her two daughters, having sold her beloved home in Homer, Alaska. Johanna and I had three vital commonalities: passports, RVs and a dose of irreverence.

Decade birthdays had never mattered. I breezed through thirty, forty and fifty. I expected the same of sixty. So wrong. I awoke confounded. *Get out and do something fun for yourself.* Pedicure? Massage? I decided to recolor the butterfly tattoo that adorned my left breast. Three decades had taken their toll. I would return those fleshy wings to bright orange, yellow and blue. Make proud the spirit of the black New Orleans Goddess who welcomed a trade of a photo print: a butterfly for a saguaro cactus landscape. Back then tats were hearts on the Army dudes, motorcycle gang members or ex-cons.

I biked excitedly through rain to a tattoo parlor. *Sorry, we're booked for the day* so I pedaled miles downtown to another. The sign said "Open Saturdays" but it was Saturday and they were closed. I stood by the door, willing it to unlock.

60, so round said a Taos-sista. I'd worked damned hard to meet it with vigor and good health, ensuring an entry with panache. Facebook messages flooded my wall, heartfelt emails in my inbox; poems and phone calls peppered my day. It was me who let me down, but that was about to change.

Surprise!

I walked through Johanna's door and into a rowdy roomful of RV comrades. Felicity had found care for her elderly mother and made her way from Twin Falls. Dar had layered mascara onto her thick lashes and laughed a hearty hello through the doorway. Trig just happened to land in Boise and said *Sure thing, I'll be there!* Six women blasting "Row Row Row Your Boat" through plastic kazoos. The ultimate Zen-zany song. No better group to kick my butt over the threshold of sixty. We'd shared kayaks and parties while wintering on the beach of Lake Havasu, but no night ever topped the memorable drunken-dames-around-the-campfire night.

Bocce ball was over and the food table picked clean as a dozen of us circled our camp chairs close to the campfire flame. Wine flowed. Cackles split the night. After a quick go around on ex-husbands (editorial comments welcomed) we moved on to the challenge of declaring our number of lovers. Around the circle we went to oohs & ahhs. Six. Thirteen. Three (*liar!*). The average number would have stayed under ten were it not for a handful of us that raised the bar. Thirty-one was the number to beat. Last to speak was seventy year old, white-haired Felicity. *One hundred and ten* she blurted as the rest of us crowed. *Hey, it was the 60's! – a fuck was a handshake!* Epitaphs come in many forms.

I closed in on "Where the West Still Lives" Mancos. The Sleeping Ute's mountain plateau stretched across the distance as the significance of my full circle came to bear. I'd done it: hitched my trailer to a pickup and in RV lingo, rubber tramped it to Alaska. I wanted a Quest badge that read "Sixty Sexy Solo." Not Botox 'n tummy-tuck sexy, mind you. Sexy as in wrinkles that hollered *viva!* Love slave to passionate purpose, trailing truth down the freedom road.

The snowline dipped ominously low. Sharkstooth Pass, where I'd stood on the cusp of departure, was cloaked in white. I was back, but my spirit wasn't so sure. Spirit and I, we'd been on the road for five months. She needed some repetition before she would trust that stop was stop; that the circle was closed. Or was it? My retinas relaxed against the tawny turn of fall. I cherished autumn; couldn't wait to find an aspen grove and lie down against her honey heart, when leaves let go in a blizzard blast to earth.

I headed nervously toward Casa Barnyard, the farm apartment Jay and I had shared. I yearned to see Pooka and wasn't sure if Jay would be part of the package. I'd called ahead and left a message. He thankfully wasn't there, leaving me with Pooka time. I called for her and scanned the yard and corrals. No Pooka. I called again. Several anxious minutes passed before she leapt from the window of an old horse trailer and made a beeline to my arms. I lay down on my belly and greeted her eye to eye.

She followed me like a shadow. We went for our ritualized walk, and just like old times, she mewed to be picked up about a quarter mile down the road. I lifted and swung her onto my shoulders; held onto her tail in our familiar precarious game of balance. Eventually she climbed onto my back, her signal that she was ready to jump onto the road and walk again. I bent at my waist to provide a platform for her to leap, but she didn't. She sat upright on my back and held me bent in place. I wiggled. She would not budge. I'd left her behind and she had something to say about it. Ten minutes passed. She and I, frozen in place.

Our bonding ritual complete, we eventually made it back that day. She talked in peep purrs I'd not heard before. Then she walked to the door and looked back at me. *Follow me* she mewed. She wanted me in that house again. Like old times. I rose, loaded Teak into Blue and performed my best job of backing the trailer yet. I stepped on the gas, drove a short way, stopped and looked back. Pooka sat by that door. Sunlight etched her golden leopard-spotted flecks. *I'll be back. We'll soon hit the road.*

I was parked a few blocks from daughter Hope on a vacant lot off a dead-end gravel street. I had camped there before, within earshot of the tiny Mancos River and the chirpy birds that frequented the cottonwood bosque. It was grand to be back, awash in mother-daughter time. Hope whipped up a birthday meal of Mediterranean pork with a sizzling olive, raisin and balsamic vinegar sauce; a spice cake with maple syrup frosting. We met every day – walked our dogs, watched football and movies; talked and laughed heart to heart. We indulged in our favorite fun, hitting garage sales. Hope snagged a couple of wine glasses for a quarter and I put down $3.00 for a sleek sexy dress. Fun to wonder what circumstances would pull that dress onto my body. Halloween, most likely.

A package arrived at Hope's door addressed to me. It was from Carole: a hand-quilted pillow of songbirds and owls and shiny golden suns and stars. My 60th birthday present.

I arranged a time to meet Jay at the casa. I looked forward to seeing him, to sit and catch up. I knocked on the door and no answer. No Jay, no Pooka. I called him on my cell and got voicemail. He'd stood me up. I swallowed anger and set up another meeting via email. No apology or explanation. Shades of old times.

Next time he met me at the door with a clipped hello and a hasty demand that I move. *Leave* he demanded *or I'll throw your things off the balcony. The sheriff lives just over there.* He pointed and threatened to get a restraining order. Shocked didn't begin to describe. I hadn't seen him in months; our sparse communications had been friendly. Furthermore, we had agreed I could store possessions in a closet. That's when he blurted *Pooka is mine!*

Let's not do this I said. *You know she's my cat.*

He followed my every move as I walked to my closet. A woman's robe hung on my former hook. The picture clarified. Then I noticed a huge dowel in the track of the glass sliding door. Did he really think I'd climb the wall to the balcony and try to break in?

You're going to make me get a lawyer to have my cat?

Welcome to divorce quipped a friend.

I spoke to a lawyer. It went like this: Being right, even legal, didn't matter. I could spend five or six grand in court and still lose Pooka because it came down to one judge who would not know the story of her life and mine and could care less that our dreams interlaced. Jay had possession. He had outmaneuvered me. *Let's get friends and go steal her back!* coaxed a sista. We would have had a lot of help.

My response was distraction. I spoke at the Mancos Library on the subject of "Sacred Place, Holy Wild: Caught in the Spiritual Crosshairs." I followed with a workshop for women, diving deeper into the confluence of soul and the earth. I was a guest on the local radio station, sharing tales and introducing my forthcoming book.

I sat in Perla, green chile beef stew simmering in the slow cooker. It was a quiet, breezeless sundown. Down the road a ways, a wild turkey scavenged for acorns along the Mancos River. I rose and stepped outside to glass the large hen; her movement seemed askew. I fiddled with the focus and gasped. She had an arrow through her breast. It stuck out both sides as she ate. Yet she followed along with her flock; flew into the cottonwood trees to roost at night.

Lynn helped me move the large items out of Casa Barnyard as Jay glared on. Pooka wasn't in sight. I held to our agreement on how to split things and later wondered why I was so honest. Lynn had offered me a storage shed on her property and many items went to Hope. We topped off the day with Alaska salmon from my freezer with cream cheese, bagels and a bottle of champagne.

I was elated and exhausted. A melancholy edginess crept in as winter drew closer. Notions of staying through the holidays evaporated with colder nighttime temps and Perla's plastic pipes. It was decision time and my decision was no, I would not winterize Perla and rent a place to live. This quest was young. With no particular destination in mind, sixty sexy solo was rarin' to hit the road.

I shifted Blue into 4WD as Hope and I climbed the serpentine, snow-covered road. We were off to cut a Solstice tree, giggle-jabbering our way through a ritual we had kept alive since she was a toddler. I waded excitedly through thigh-deep powder. Sensible Hope stayed closer to the road. She found a soft needled fir that was growing inches from another, a spindly six feet tall. Cutting it would free the other to grow. I grabbed the teensy-trusty McGuckin's Hardware saw I'd carried for twenty years. We thanked the tree for her gift as I knelt under the boughs and sawed away. Elated, we dragged her to the road and lifted her into Blue's backend; high-fived our feat. Decorations awaited in Hope's homey abode. It was eggnog time with a pinch of sadness. My departure was imminent. No more daily daughter.

Here we go again, Teak. We pulled onto the highway. Acceleration was slow as my gas pedal foot met my heart's resistance. I loved this little town. Goodbye Absolute Bakery. Goodbye butcher in the little grocery store. We passed Teak's favorite park and the local herd of yaks. We topped the hill and neared the turnoff for Casa Barnyard and Pooka. Sad turned mad as I pounded on the steering wheel; it was all I could do to not throw up. Or turn down that road. Bastard.

I sought a secluded boondock at Natural Bridges National Monument, an easy half day away. Teak and I had the one-way loop to ourselves on the warm December tanktop-day. Perla towed silently behind as I scouted an off-road place to park for the night. The nausea of losing Pooka did not cease. I was still close, should I go back? My mind chattered as I passed the park campground in favor of a cottonwood-studded wash.

The sun freefell toward night. I biked up a dirt road as Teak ran alongside. We stopped on a red rock outcropping, the air still as death. No birdsong, no aromas, no wild signs. It was Teak and me and a narrow sandstone bridge blood red with sunset. *Best dog in the world.* Her brown eyes found my blues.

Natural Bridges. No place better to bridge recent loss with the foggy future. A chill enveloped my body as a coyote yip ripped the air. I turned to see the opal moon lift above the cliffs; rubbed Teak behind the ears. Karma would take care of Jay. And that turkey had shown me that one could do quite well with an arrow through the breast. I breathed deep the freedom air. Alone, but not lonely, in uninterrupted space.

The evolving plan included piñatas, beach and vibrant colors, but for now I was in womad-mode, skimming the periphery of Monument Valley, in concert with past cowboys, Indians, explorers, mountain men and more recently, hobos. Women, too, were nomads. For centuries, our hearth was a moving one, unchained from a static home. I wondered what spiritual price today's women paid to be fixed in place. Rudyard was right. *Some stay home. Some don't.* Those that don't were growing in number, jumping tracks and living dreams, discovering parts of themselves heretofore unlived.

Monument Valley's rubicund miles loosed my rolling mind. Her spires jarred the flat dusty earth Haunted, windswept canyons kept secrets, even from the most driven historians and womads.

Tam proposed we meet in Mexico for the winter. He was in Florida with a friend whose wife had died; his grieving buddy had stopped drinking and Tam claimed to have cut way back. His voice on the phone opened my heart. Perhaps his friend's abstinence had rubbed off; long, sandy beaches might soothe his soul and turn the tide. My memory landed on our good times. A sober Tam would be a fun diversion after morning writing. He'd drive his own vehicle, ensuring my autonomy. I agreed.

That night I dreamt Pooka was living in a hole with two downy baby nighthawks. One by one they came out of the hole and hopped around; sweet innocence. Pooka followed them out, thrust herself high in the air and came at me like a fly ball. *Catch me, here I am!* I broke her fall but she slipped through my hands. Jay walked into the scene. He grabbed Pooka and ignored me, finality rendered.

Crossing into Mexico had always been easy. One enters the border area, stops and faces a green or red light. Green means hi, howdy, keep going. Red signals pull over for questions and possible search. I got the green as I headed for the next checkpoint a few miles down the road. The soldiers took their time; kept peering in the windows. They couldn't believe I was driving a truck and towing a trailer alone. *Solo?* they kept asking, shaking their heads, looking half bewildered, half impressed.

Si! I said casting them a killer smile. Sixty sexy solo.

The swaying palms of Islandia were a soothing sight. As a rule I shied away from RV parks – too many people too close. I hadn't boondocked in Mexico since the Baja, years ago, when circumstances were safer and I was paired up. I preferred RV parks with little infrastructure, ones that attracted people who didn't need to be entertained. I had a special place in my heart for quaint Islandia in Old Kino Bay. I'd rented a casita in the past with friends. This was the first time I'd showed up towing. Tam followed me in his van and stepped out to help decide on a space. He disagreed with my choice. It didn't bode well.

I parked where the muse would be happy, adjacent to the beach with a clear view of the Mexican scene. Kids played and flew kites as fishermen awaited the next forceful wave to bring their *pangas* to shore. Within sight of the picturesque stone boat ramp, I was witness to many endearing scenes, from quinceañera photo shoots to sundown lovers entwined in a kiss. Real Mexico.

Islandia was rich in tales and gringo neighbors, with fervent right-wing politicos and the squabbles of any small community. I parked on the far end, down a small hill and away from the long-term RVers, putting distance between myself and the buzz. I was with the short-term travelers; a fun turnover of vagabonds traveling north to south and back again. Characters all.

I nuzzled into the smell of Tam; our sex burned the bed. The honeymoon, however, was brief. Turned out the lazy, sun-drenched beach plunked him into drinking-vacation mode. To top it off, he couldn't tolerate my need for uninterrupted writing space. Nope, this would not do. The high drama of the sea was unacceptable here. I was not trapped on a boat. Nothing would interfere with finishing my book.

Thirty pages. Sixty pages. I wrote like a madwoman. *You've got to be lead dog* he accused. Yes, in fact, I did. Author in writing mode. Gin his mistress, the muse was mine. Done by noon; the afternoon was free to bike and explore. We walked distant beaches and took in nature's surprises: two whales and my first sighting of Brandt's Geese. We grilled his daily catch; sautéed fresh shrimp in tequila, butter and lime. Drunk drama, however, commenced with sunset. My gay neighbors kept an eye on my welfare. One of them was a non-drinking alcoholic; he saw reality with eagle eyes.

I want to change said Tam. I believed him. But all of the talk and promises brought no progress. I was unapologetic: couples must bring out the best in one another. He complained that I was talking to Hope too much on the internet. I didn't take the bait and we cruised by the rough spot into distant desert landscape, rich with *cardón* cactus, Great Blue Herons, Black Vultures and Osprey. We picnicked on the beach as he reeled in one fish after another. We returned to Perla where tipsy Tam disappeared into a car with others for dinner. A small thing, but oh, that familiar *SNAP!* He returned that night with a peace offering of green chiles.

It's over. I want you gone in the morning I said.

I didn't spend two grand to come down here and be evicted he said.

No discussion. No negotiation. The writing womad had spoken.

It may have been right, it was certainly necessary, but it wasn't easy. He rose at dawn, packed his van and left without saying goodbye. I numbed with angst and anger. Sadness tore my heart; but there was no *you should have known better.* I had done my best. I had given a special man another chance. I stood alone at ocean's edge, a book to finish, another boat full of grief to unload. *Sink those toes into the sand, Christina, and face out to sea*. My free wheelin' life was mine again.

Up at dawn to write, I stuck my head outdoors mid-morning. I sat on Perla's step, laced my sneakers and walked three, four and eventually six miles along the beach, as if one could outwalk heartache. Then one day, out of earshot, alone with the sea, I did something I'd never done before: I loosed a deep guttural laugh into the salt-laden wind.

It was a forced fake laugh that belched the air right out of me. It felt odd at first but I kept it up. It became easier with practice and it felt great to access unreachable places. I envisioned a lump of energy, a spontaneous release of pain, ejected through laughter, and with it, the sadness of Tam. Of Pooka. And it worked. Fake laughter eventually led to real laughter. Real laughter led to chemical feel-good changes in the brain. And through it all, the glob of grief moved on.

I followed the laugh-walk with stretches. All senses awake, my body absorbed the salt sea milieu. I delighted in lines of Brown Pelicans wing dancing above the waves; the foamy tideline of sea treasures left behind by the moon's pull. I took refuge in a small pocket of beach where waves carried thousands of shells to the sand, rolled them over and over as the sea receded. My secret rainstick; a soft jingle jungle that soothed the nerves.

It became easier and easier to laugh on demand after a few days. All I had to do was imagine what anyone might think if they happened to hear me. I swore I heard the ocean whisper *she who laughs, lasts.*

The full moon turned egg yolk yellow and lowered herself upon the sea. I dreamed that Tam and I were hiking up a mountain looking for the trail. I broke away and threaded through boulders steep and dangerous to the top. Forced to leap or turn around, I leapt and discovered the right path. *I found it! This way!* I said. He stood stone cold. *Get rid of me* he said. *Yes* I answered.

I rose and kayaked to Alcatraz Island. Took to the island shore and walked among pilot whale bones; offered silent blessings. Asked to be worthy of blessings in return.

Imbolc, Candlemas or Groundhog Day – whichever way you cut it, the light returns. Glory be, early spring is in the air. Play the Beatles *Here Comes the Sun*! I dreamed of leaping ocelots as I kept my nose to the grindstone and fingers to the keyboard: write, belly laugh, sundowners with neighbors, early to bed, get up and write again.

Two weeks later Solo Sojourner typed THE END! I sprang from the laptop and let loose with a holler. It was Valentine's Day. I donned a white linen skirt that flowed with the ocean breeze and took to the beach. Low-flying sea birds whizzed by to join others in the distance. I jogged to catch the commotion. An ethereal cloud of wing and floating birds moved amoeba-like against the sun-drenched backdrop of Alcatraz Island. I stood mesmerized as thousands of gulls, cormorants and pelicans dove and screamed offshore in a feeding frenzy. A climax of mouth-dropping energy. And just like that, the ecstatic dance stopped. The sea ghosts dispersed in watery directions, their fishy breakfast gone.

A glistening half-submerged shell caught my eye. I pulled it from the sand. It was a translucent, fist-sized heart. A valentine from the sea! I plopped cross-legged on the sand and wept; stared across to those island whale bones as Teak nudged my arm.

I returned to Perla, unlocked the door and entered my writing sanctum. My laptop sat open on the table. The finished book glared on the screen. Oh Lordy, this would take time to sink in. No more daily note taking; done with paragraph deliberations. No more winnowing; searching for just the right/write word. The weighty anxiety of an unfinished story disappeared. I let loose a yell and jumped outside.

Word spread fast through little Islandia. That night friends piled into Randolph's car, the largest at the RV park, and he drove us to New Kino for seafood at seaside and margaritas all around. Then back we came to Old Kino and a local seedy bar. Tecates led to mescal shots. Mariachi and ranchero tunes blasted away on the old jukebox and we took to the tabletops to dance. Well, I did. I don't recall that anyone followed me.

On a scale of one to ten my hangover was a six. I gulped some water, downed a couple vitamin Bs and stepped outside to find my sneakers gone. I glanced inside and did a double take. Nope, filched, I guessed, by the same person who had stood on a chair, slid open a window and pinched my prized German knife from the dish drainer. It was an inglorious week at the camp. A bike was stolen from a camper a few moments after arrival and someone else's computer went bye-bye from her kitchen table.

This was the hard part of Mexico. For all her vivacious energy and warm-heartedness, she was a culture on the edge, especially since the cartels had scared away tourism. I chose Old Kino over the condo-studded Anglo beaches and gated communities. I preferred to be part of the local rituals as I watched fishermen board their *pangas* in the morning and head into the watery dawn. As hard as their lives were, I never once saw them lose their tempers. They always had time to help one another and did so with smiles and civility.

Nature abhors a vacuum, especially in the spring. So it was she sent Tracy, who floated in on a dinghy from a sleek catamaran anchored off shore. I watched as the tanned muscled man dragged the rubber raft onto sand adjacent to my trailer. Dressed in my good luck white linen, I made my way to the beach. *Can I help you?* He looked up with a warm smile; asked for directions to a *tienda* where he might restock. I gave directions and he followed up with an offer I couldn't refuse. I donned my tour guide cap for the day and he picked up the tab as I showed him around town. We drove around the bay to distant beaches, the estuary for a fresh oyster lunch, *tiendas* and hardware stores. We swilled margaritas, savored fresh shrimp as the sun fell behind pelican silhouettes. It was a fun and gracious day, smattered with fascinating stories from my nautical friend. No overnight stays;

just a wink from the Goddess who let me know that anything is possible. And then She followed up with Jake.

I met old Mike, first. His dog. Jake was from Tucson and managed a condo on the beach in New Kino. I had noticed him on his patio every morning when I walked. One morning I waved and he motioned me up. I made my way uphill through thick hot sand, took a seat at his table as he poured fresh orange juice. It turned into a regular ritual as we talked Kierkegaard, climate change and *The Alchemist*. I liked Jake. A lot. He was witty and sharp. Before long he showed up at Perla with gifts of fresh crab and shrimp. We expanded our time to bike rides and hikes to distant beaches but never moved beyond platonic hugs. Unless you count the night I saved his life.

We had joined another couple at a family-owned café known for its *carne asada*, dried beef akin to jerky. We were downing margaritas and chewing away when Jake suddenly grabbed my hand and squeezed. He reached for his throat. *I can't breathe.* I jumped up, grabbed my blue-faced friend and pulled him a few steps to the deck. *Hold on* I ordered and placed his hands on the railing. The long-ago CPR class flashed before my eyes as I took the palm of my hand and walloped him between the shoulder blades. Out flew the meat, a healthy spurt of whatever and a gasp for air. No Heimlich required.

Never a late-night person – yes, I've missed my share of terrific parties – I declined an invitation to party on. He walked me to Perla's door; held me in a close embrace.

Keep smiling he said.

It's easy to smile when you show up.

You give me too much credit, Christina.

We couldn't stop waving as he drove out of sight. Sadness overtook me. That was the last night I saw Jake. He departed for

Tucson the next day and by the time he returned I was gone. I didn't want to lose touch, but I'd never learned his last name.

My days in Kino wound down. It was time to leave the Black Vultures that picked bones clean. The Brandt's Geese, wading Willets and spirit-lifting Roseate Spoonbills. The lines of Brown Pelicans that drifted effortlessly along sand dune contours. My body would no longer pulse with the tides. Yes, time to depart: my Colgate toothpaste tube was all squeezed out.

I made the rounds to say goodbye, intent on catching Maryam, the office manager. Maryam's plump body was wrapped head to toe in colorful silk, her short presence covered in Muslim fashion. This young Mexican woman had grabbed my heart from the sultry day I'd met her, when she told me her story in broken English. She said she had once been a teenage party girl. I imagined how beautiful she had been, her dark skin, hair and movie star smile. By her early twenties, however, her life felt pointless. Bars and shopping did not fulfill her spirit. She began to secretly study Islam and to learn Arabic.

How did this happen? There were no Muslims in Kino Bay. No mosque. The nearest Muslims were seventy miles by bus in Hermosillo. The more she studied, however, the more she felt in tune with the teachings. After two years of study and prayer she converted, went public and began to wear her full hijab. She risked everything. Her family, friends and employer were shocked. In time, however, they accepted her decision.

Maryam eventually met her husband-to-be, who was from Morocco, online. At first she resisted his romantic overtures but he persisted and eventually won her love. Once they cleared a series of strict religious hoops they married via Skype, never having met in person. He left his family and moved to Kino, knowing no Spanish. What courage!

I'd attended their humble wedding reception. They were the sweetest couple.

I had traveled solo in Mexico and Guatemala, Honduras and Nicaragua, for thirty years. I'd flown, taken third class buses piled high with chicken crates, driven, camped and hitchhiked. I had found my excursions south of the US border to be exciting, touching encounters with the people. Although safety concerns had increased with the cartels, common sense went a long way. I no longer camped in remote places, I was more careful about solo beach walks and did not drive at night or early morning, when cows and other unsavory possibilities ambled dark roads.

My good Mexican karma riding shotgun, I departed Kino Bay and picked up the toll road north at Hermosillo. I was accustomed to highway checks by machine-gun-carrying soldiers who appeared to be sixteen years old. These guys were always friendly and waved me on. I was not prepared, however, for the soldiers who stood beside the toll booth, holding guns and plastic buckets. *Buenos días* I said as I tossed my toll money in their bucket. Uh, keep the change. Highway robbery with a *grácias*. The men waved their arms to keep me moving. *No problemo.* I laughed and hastily headed up the road. *Solamente en México.*

Three nights later I was back in Cortez. I unhitched under a shade tree at Lynn's where I off-loaded beach gear and Christmas decorations and picked up cool weather clothing. A short stop, but long enough to experience a revelation. I was driving down a side street in Cortez and a dark green CR-V came toward me. I did a double take as the car and driver registered. It was Jay. He didn't recognize the truck. He was gone in a few seconds, like an apparition.

I felt no anger. No regret. It was over. I would not attempt to collect Pooka. I soon departed for a summer stay at Carole's, with a planned check-out-Pat stop in Creston, British Columbia. I'd met him in my final days at Kino. We were both heading north and he invited me to stop and stay.

I camped the first night along the gentle red rock lined Colorado River outside of Moab. The second night I walked with the birds along the Great Salt Lake. Travel north was glitch free. I remembered to tuck in the stairs. No open vents flapped in the wind. I didn't forget to take the pictures off the wall.

I gingerly pulled into an out-of-way Idaho Quick Stop to feed my licorice craving. I watched as a tight-jeaned beauty in cowboy boots strode out the door and jumped into her cherry red Dodge Ram pickup. That's when I saw the bumper sticker: "If you're gonna ride my ass you'd better be pulling my hair." Ya! I snapped a photo. Sexy solo and ooooh, I'd guess thirty.

June's new moon eclipse hit hard. My friend Emilie's cat Sandino disappeared and Carole had a nightmare that her grandkids didn't know her. I wasn't immune either: I showed up at my friend Pat's home in Creston to discover he lived with his mother. He called her sweetheart and he lived in her basement surrounded by hockey jerseys and photos from his high school days. This was going to be a short stop, but not short enough.

Pat and I headed to Kootenay Lake with his boat. The put-in was at the end of a gravel road. We parked his old pickup and boat trailer and Teak and I walked toward Pat's motorboat on the perfect-weather day. *No need to bring your purse. We'll lock it in the truck.*

I felt uneasy. I was carrying more cash than usual and some favorite silver earrings. I weighed the choices: risk a waterlogged purse in the boat or leave my valuables in the old radio-less pickup truck that would hardly attract thieves. Pat called me paranoid. I acquiesced. It was safe-and-sound Canada, after all, home of the Mounties.

We returned four hours later to a broken rear window, complements of the tire iron in the bed of the truck. My purse, hidden deeply under the seat, was all that was taken. Shock morphed into anger: at myself, at Pat, and OH-Can-a-DUH. I could not get over the fact that I had traveled the world for thirty years, across oceans and into the depths of the Third World and had never had a serious incident. It took civil Canada to steal my identity. It felt like a set-up.

My driver's license was kaput, tossed somewhere in a ditch or in the hands of someone with my sparkling silver dangles through her lobes. I ordered a new one and set up a mailing address at the Idaho border crossing store. I'd pick up the replacement in a month, when I headed south. Until then I drove without a license and carried the police report with me.

I loaded Teak the next day and headed east out of Creston, the only direction I hadn't explored thus far. I'd zipped along at 70-mph for thirty minutes when I spied a country cemetery. Old graveyards calmed my spirit; epitaphs were fascinating fun. I slowed Blue as a sharp squeal emanated from underneath. *Oh geez* I exhaled. *Not something else.* A quick look at the tires and a walk-around garnered no clues. I continued up the road.

I braked twenty minutes later and the squeal repeated. Worried the bearings were going out, I turned around, but not before I bit on a yard sale sign. I was walking toward the sale when I heard the raspy squeal again. Nope. Not the brakes.

I scooted underneath on my back and there, huddled into the only space large enough on Blue's frame, was a teensy golden kitten. I reached for her and she leapt. She scurried through the woods, stopped at a stream and lapped feverishly before she jumped in and swam upstream. This was not just any cat.

I returned to the sale and paid Sandra two bucks for a throw rug. She said the kitten wouldn't last the night with all of the hungry critters about. Then I made a move that defied all common sense. I took out a business card and handed it to her. *If she shows up, please call me.*

I awoke with a dream of the kitten around midnight. The next morning my phone rang at 7:30. *The kitten is here* said Sandra. *It showed up meowing beneath our bedroom window at midnight.* I smiled. *I'll be right there.*

I returned to the house on the edge of the forest. The long-haired golden hitchhiker could not have been over four weeks old. She had made herself at home in their garage, sleeping on the couch. I picked her up and whoops! – felt two little knobs beneath the tail. *His* eyes were matted with yellow gunk, his sinuses were congested and he sneezed. His marmalade coat was scruffy as heck. I had sworn I would never have a long-haired cat. The danger of saying *never*. I named him Hobo.

I packed, hooked up and pointed north to Kaslo, a bag of juicy Jonathans on the front seat. My stomach flip-flopped as I accelerated past the turnoff for the boat launch. I wondered about the short meeting with Pat and the theft. I sorely missed my silver earrings from Taxco. I'd had them for decades. On the other hand, Hobo and I had united, and I could sure use some laugh-out-loud kitten energy.

Crossing paths with a stranger could be short, simple or life-changing. I'd once shown a grateful woman how to stuff pillows into the RV-cupboard so the glasses didn't tip and break. I'd introduced one man to the color turquoise. Another had never tasted an avocado. (*Really? And you're sixty?)* And forty years later, I couldn't look at an artichoke without remembering the lover who had cooked my first.

It wasn't always obvious why someone dropped into my life. I trusted, however, that every road brought me closer to an undefinable home ... identity theft included. While my loss was flagrant, what of the women whose identities were slowly stolen by unhealthy relationships; their career paths detoured? What identity theft was worse than to walk through the same door for decades into a routine, soul-deadening job?

This personal loss hardly seemed fair given I'd already shed roles and was flying in the face of the ordinary. *Fair, Christina? ... Stop whining and savor the irony. Carry on, Womad.*

I clicked Blue into 4WD and began the steep ascent up the gravel lane to Chris and Carole's. They had arranged a pull-off parking spot that perched on the mountainside, twenty yards below their house. Chris' biceps were just the ticket as he turned Perla's large crank to raise the trailer off the ball. I placed wooden blocks under the hitch, liberated Teak and Hobo and we turned for the house. I melted into the deck chair as Carole handed me a Blue Sapphire gin and tonic. *A toast to us!* – clink – as I looked down on Perla and saw smoke.

I tore down the hill. Carole followed with the hose as the fire spread beneath the trailer. We sprayed in a panic and drenched the flame. Turned out when Chris lowered the trailer the emergency break-away cable had gotten caught underneath the blocks. I was tired and distracted; missed it completely. The tautness simulated a disconnect from the truck and engaged the brakes; became so hot it started to burn. Holy cow, strange things were happening.

Teak, Hobo and I stayed for several weeks as I sent out book queries and repaired the trailer with the help of my remote angel, Philip. *Get under the truck and send me photos*. He directed me to snip here and tape there. Meanwhile, Carole and I cleared Hobo's matted eyes with homeopathic remedies. He took to the litter box in a snap and rode on my shoulder like a parrot. He looked into my eyes as if he understood every word I spoke. Teak was indifferent. Hobo was fearless, drinking Teak's water and swiping a paw at her leg when she passed by. And with one ring of the phone, it appeared he had brought me the greatest of luck.

It was an agent, a past managing editor of a top publishing house, and she wanted to represent *Drive Me Wild*. She said I was a brand. *We'll land movie rights and a book contract.* I was certain that after twenty years of persistent writing, two published books and mountains of rejections letters, my ship had come in.

I was perusing Helen Fisher's website to read up on her latest anthropological findings. I'd followed her research since my Boulder years as a women's psychotherapist, in agreement with her findings on biology and relationship. She believed that humans were not biologically programmed for long-term monogamous relationships. The biological imperative was to have several mates to ensure robust bloodlines. I'd found her research borne out again and again on personal and professional levels.

I clicked on a link in the middle of an article, expecting it to take me to more information. Instead I found myself on a dating site called *Chemistry* that was based upon her studies and promoted by her. I was intrigued. I'd never joined a dating site. I signed up and paid for a month; figured if nothing else, my experience might make an interesting article.

Chemistry was tired of me in a couple of days. I kept pushing the "not really" button when they sent new contacts. The site prompted me for a reason, but their drop-down list didn't include options like "he says he's 59 but he looks like an old fart." Okay. So I was a finicky bitch. Did they add that to my profile in invisible ink? What peeved me most were contacts without pictures. C'mon, chemistry without photos? A man messaged and said to contact him if I got bored. I told him I didn't get bored, I got curious.

It was a two-hand squeeze on the toothpaste tube as my long brown hair fell into my face. Espresso bubbled away as the sun broke over the Purcell Mountains. I didn't get lonely but I did have longings. I'd been told my body tasted sweet. Olfactory had everything to do with how I responded to a man. And his smile. And his eyes. And the way he walked. And the cadence of his voice. And there I sat, staring at a computer screen perusing blurry photos.

I pictured myself in a cabin by water and aspen trees in full autumn color. A partner to love and rowdy around with. I vowed not to go beyond one month with the online dating world. I had opened a window and someone might crawl through. A pilot in Boise popped up on the screen the day I changed my mail/male forward to Boise in preparation for my southern migration. Perhaps we'd meet for iced coffee at a sidewalk cafe. Meanwhile I was having fun with emails from a Montana backwoodsman who kept me laughing from a distance.

The intensity of the times was palpable; all of my close friends were in one form of upheaval or another. Alice, who had once cut my hair in Todos Santos, lay upon her Taos bed, in and out of consciousness, drifting toward death. It was my first death-through-Facebook experience and I wasn't sure what to think. Her friends took turns to sit and read the river of non-stop Facebook messages, expressions of love, reverence and respect. Words to carry her soul to the other side.

Another friend was catapulted into capitulation and heartbreak by a text that mistakenly popped up on her phone revealing her daughter's abortion. An Idaho sister recovered from her daughter's death, heartbroken with the memory of a liver transplant that couldn't happen in time. Alexandra departed on a cross country road trip with her husband who was in the throes of brain cancer as Johanna struggled minute to minute with nicotine withdrawal. She prayed that tossing cigarettes at age seventy would make a difference in the number of sunsets she would witness. All of this, as Ellen, her husband, kids and horses, were kicked off their foreclosed farm.

I solemnly pieced these sister-tales together, thankful for my six-week layover on Carole's land. We sat at her table, sipped wine and jabbered away. Then one night she suddenly looked up: *It's ready!* She had drawn me a hot bath; added rose petal bubble bath. No one had done that since a Taos lover many years ago. We had made soft long love as shadows melted down adobe walls. Then he rose and ran a bubble bath. He took my hand and lowered me into a warm tub at sun's final blush.

What to do when calamity coalesced? Chris baked peach pies; Carole met with homeopathy patients. I typed away, giggling at a kitten who teeter-tottered between love, light and Cujo. As times intensified we did well to cuddle up to comrades. Run bubble baths for one another. Or, go to nature.

It didn't take a scientist to tell us forests made us feel good, but it took Japanese studies to discover why trees improved our health and state of mind. Trees emit a protective chemical called phytoncide; it lowers blood pressure and pulse rate, stabilizes cortisol and increases white blood cells. The Japanese call walking in the trees *shinrin-yoku*, forest bathing. It was the most natural thing in the world to stop by a tree, take off my shoes and sit. Feet on the ground and no rubber sole barrier, the earth's electrons passed from earth to body, attacking the stress-induced free radicals, those nasty cells that wreak havoc, cause cancer.

Trees and me. Many a time I leaned against bark and sensed the transference of energy. It felt like a healing. Like magic, trees absorbed and transformed energy, turned slugfest to lovefest. Trees are one of the oldest, wisest beings on the planet. A particular aspen clone is believed to be the largest living organism on earth.

Communion with wild nature, be it trees, mountains or celestial bodies, has taken many forms through the ages. Moon-and sun-driven rituals of fertility, eroticism and sacred rites had long offered fluids on the altar of the earth: tears, snot, menstrual blood, saliva, vaginal juice. That we have pushed an intimate relationship with nature aside comes at great cost. Metaphorical lover or otherwise, this I knew: orgasmic contact with other life forms was essential for oneness. Kiss the earth however one pleased, through poetry or dance, song or prayer. The wild recognized this vibration and responded. Healing resided in untamed places. We needed only to show up and receive.

I snipped a few pink cosmos and Black-eyed Susans, set them on Perla's small table and lit a candle. Hobo attacked my right-hand fingers as the pen began to move. All writing began with willy-nilly scribbles in my journal. Confidential corners were imperative to speak the unspeakable; practice for the outer world.

This day I was buoyed by the impending reunion with Kathryn. We'd met thirty years ago in the sweat-stinky Managua airport during the Sandinista war. I had hitchhiked throughout the country to photograph the revolutionary murals and get a pulse for Reagan's Contra conflict. It was a hard place to be, but not as hard as Kathryn's magazine assignment to cover the nuns who had been brutally murdered in El Salvador.

She and I were in the departure line headed back to the USA. All was well until the ticket man asked for the exit tax in Nica dollars. I'd given my last cent and two roles of film to the taxi driver as a tip. He'd driven me to the top of Masaya volcano outside of Managua, and I was happy to empty my pockets for him; but now I couldn't leave the country and would miss my plane. I was close to tears when a Goddess with waist-long golden hair stepped forward in her sundress and sequined sandals and offered to pay the ten dollars. Friends forever. That night we roomed next to one another in Guatemala City and had stayed in contact ever since.

Now, decades later, Kathryn was flying to Missoula to visit an aunt and we agreed to meet halfway between there and Kaslo. I contacted Bud, the *Chemistry* site guy in Montana, to set up a coffee date along the way. He was game. Then Kathryn contracted bronchitis and called off our rendezvous. My get well prayers went unanswered as Bud bemoaned the fact that "the bait to get me thar has disappeared."

I'd like to hear your voice, would you like to hear mine? I typed. I called and left a message. Bud called back and did the same, saying that I sounded *pret...tee dy...nam...ic.* He spoke with a twang somewhere between *Deliverance* and my Texas cousin. We decided to meet in Bonners Ferry, Bombers Ferry to Bud, a reference to Ruby Ridge. I suggested a picnic by the Kootenai River at a little grassy park I'd recently discovered. We'd bring the dogs. In three days.

Carole and I waxed zany over my venture into terra incognito. Was that dark shadowed photo really him? I gave Carole my contact information as we agreed I should not make a plan; leave it open, see how things fly. Pack a bag? We joked about the days when we always packed a bag in case we got laid. Now we packed bags in case we got DE-layed.

Bud and I met at a bakery at a highway intersection. I was an hour late thanks to the backup at the border. I pulled into the sun-drenched parking lot, turned off the ignition and took a deep breath as I studied the man sitting quietly at a picnic table. He wore a t-shirt and black jeans with black suspenders. There was a liver-spotted hunting dog at his side. The man didn't have an inkling of Dexter vibes. I opened the door and stepped out.

We met midway on the dusty gravel with hellos. Bud and his leggy dog Boss. Christina and her sweet dog Teak. He had assured me he wasn't *fat, bald or ugly... yet*. He was modest. He possessed sky blue eyes and a smile that melted my heart. We sat outside and talked for an hour and I decided ya, let's move on to the picnic. *Doggie daycare* he said. Three more hours of talk and laughter. The sun was getting low. We didn't want it to end.

I don't know what you've planned but you're welcome to come to my place and spend some more time. I didn't tell him that I had no plan. His place was a hundred miles east in the forest, thirty miles from the nearest town. Would my cell phone work there? I pointed Blue east and followed the silhouette of his little black sports car. I dialed up Hope for backup, confident of my intuition and ability to extricate myself from situations that might twist sideways.

I had packed for an overnight; I stayed eight days. Bud's new, modest ranch-style home sat at the edge of the Fisher River, facing into mountains. The place hummed with feral possibility. It immediately matched up with my desire to sit still in a wild place of solitude.

Every day we rode double on the ATV, deeper into Bud's wild Montana landscape. He made simple, delicious meals. We visited friends, hiked, took trips into golden larch-forested mountains. Mornings began with coffee and hot tub soaks on the deck. Bohemian waxwings worked the riverside bushes; birdsong mingled with the sound of river rapids. I photographed while he practiced with his bow, readying for the upcoming hunting season and his quest for an elk. He sent shivers through my body with his piercing blue eyes.

So how's your whirlwind summer romance going? he kept asking. Our lives were as different as could be but I was intrigued by those differences. I'd always taken pride in bridging gaps, befriending those different from myself. Bud's presence had the comfort of an old t-shirt, as we struggled to figure out where to put this encounter in the context of our fiercely independent lives.

If my Florida amiga had not gotten sick this never would have happened. That's the way August was: a strange out-of-the-blue configuration. My subscription to *Chemistry* expired as I lounged contented in bed under soft down, a lover's footsteps walking up the hallway. I wondered if I could get used to that. There was only one way to find out. I returned to BC, loaded up and made my way back to Bud's.

I parked Perla between pines and bushes. My preference, at riverside, wasn't an option. His ex had parked there and that didn't turn out so well. Across the driveway from my door was the shop. Above the door was a sign: Fabricator.

I sat in Perla, heater on, the screen door open. Autumn in Montana: frost at night, sunny eighties in the daytime. Born in October, I relished the drift of falling of leaves, nature's rot and the movement of migration. In just a few days I had witnessed a moose crossing a lake, glossy black bears, deer galore and an active eagle's nest on the top of a snag.

It was paradise with an edge; a strange man-scene in this neck of the woods. Most past-prime men were divorced and single by choice. With the gusto of a mountain man frat, they had turned their libido into wood of the tree-felling kind, building bizarre creations. One had erected an open air shed for his sawmill; two stories up was a room accessible by steep ladders. Inside that room was a pool table and a view to die for. I eventually traveled up the ladders but declined the invitation to smoke a bong. Never would have made it down.

Another man took a historic, lovely log hewn cabin perched on a mountainside and dwarfed it with a deck using logs three times larger around than me. He planned a pool room on top of the deck, and a loft overhead, topped off by a glass observation room that resembled a fire lookout. I watched the levels of construction, struggling not to lose sight of the old, original cabin. Every man I met had a life that twisted sideways in one way or another, like the guy who lived on an isolated lake surrounded by old growth larch in house jam-packed with stuff. He lived like a pack rat, which probably explained the wooden porch covered with rodent droppings.

These anti-government (except when it came to disability payments), fiercely independent men were self-made engineers, craftsmen, contractors, mechanics and yes, fabricators. Most were poor and single. The few that were married or hooked up were enmeshed in rocky predicaments. Bud blanketed me with stories of women: some left with their kids in the middle of the night, some women stayed and went stark crazy. *News of a woman in the area spreads like wildfire* he said. I was in dysfunction-land, but the backwoods bunch was nothing but respectful and friendly to me. A kindhearted man with the moniker Unibomber, a tip-of-the-hat to the real guy in Idaho, penciled his book in poverty not far down the road. He had no electricity or indoor plumbing. I eventually read his manuscript and offered some edits. It was a whooper of a story.

For all my fascination, however, I could not stomach the vitriol toward wild predators; in particular, grizzlies and wolves. I'd lived in states where wolf reintroduction was an ecological and spiritual goal; recovery efforts to return the keystone species followed decades of bloodlust extermination. There I was, at ground zero. Locals blamed plummeting elk, moose and deer populations on the wild canines. Wolf hatred was on everyone's tongues as bumper stickers proclaimed "Smoke a Pack A Day" and "Shoot, Shovel, Shut-up." You would have thought there was a wolf behind every tree. Was it really about the availability of elk? To add to the wolves' recovery plight, they became the focus of all who hated the government, which included most of this neighborhood called Happy's. Wolves were symbolic of Big Brother.

I sat quietly and listened as I allowed for the fact there might be something I had overlooked. What I felt then would be borne out: under predation, game broke into smaller groups and moved swiftly. With wolves in the landscape, hunters had to work harder for kills; go off road. Wolves, like bison, grizzlies and Native Americans before them, were a preferred target down the psychopathic road called manifest destiny. Meanwhile, Hobo and I were concerned with the game invading Perla. I set mousetraps with peanut butter and waited for the metal snap in the night.

Record highs were predicted as astrologers warned of more cosmic chaos. I felt prepared for anything the universe might present, glad to be anchored at Bud's on the river with the resident beaver and swooping Kingfisher. His burned biscuits made the smoke detectors go off as we ran laughing from the house. His lovemaking was fun and porny, peppered with hair tie cock rings and novel angles. I was hopeful that landscape, work and partner might finally come together. I could see myself on the Fisher River, writing, with a partner who prized the outdoors. Alas, my Fairy Godmother winked. I was there for a reason, but that wasn't it.

Bud and I walked several miles to the confluence of two small creeks. We saw no one as our tracks melded with elk, bear, wolf and deer. The ecstatic feeling of wild Alaska returned; the edgy reality that I was smack dab in the food chain. He carried a gun everywhere he went; I walked solo every day and did not. I relied on keen senses, karma and Teak. I had been eye to eye with black bear, griz and lion. Plenty of armed men had met their demise by grizzlies who moved faster than the time it took to raise and fire their guns. My pact with nature included a declaration to friends that if I died in the wild I did not want the predator tracked and killed. If my time was up, it was up. I preferred being pooped out by a grizzly to most other death scenarios.

Light waned as my eye caught a shiny edge in the mud. I stopped, dug with my finger and pulled out an oblong silver charm engraved with the words *Amis pour la vie*. Friends for life. It reminded me of a decade ago, when I pushed an eagle feather into the bark of an old-growth ponderosa pine and hit something hard. Encased deep within was a quartz crystal two inches in length. This French charm, deep in the forest, miles from the nearest road; the crystal deep within a tree. Let the mystery be.

The following morning I woke in the dark and made my way to the beaver ponds, fifty yards upstream through the pines. It was Teak and Hobo's favorite excursion. The dam was a work of art; I had yet to see the ghost-contractors. Bud said they had showed up when I did.

Camera in hand, I sat on the chilly ground, waiting for light, shadow and action to coalesce. An elk bugle broke silence. The looooooong primal call of sex. Rifle season was two days away. It might have been a hunter checking the proximity of game. But no, this call was strong and clear with a hint of forlorn; unlike those from the lips of hunters. Another call, as waves appeared on the glassy water and a small beaver swam into view. I watched until the ripples caught the light and began to shoot.

I moved on into my daily hike. A bald eagle flew low overhead. Teak balked a mile in as she picked up a scent. We dropped into a marshy creekside with a faint two-track next to a lake called Banana. Twenty yards in I heard loud splashing. I scurried to find a window through the thickets. My eyes fell upon three frisky cow elk. They stepped out of view as a stately six-point bull emerged. Bull and harem stepped upstream in broad daylight, the river their pathway. I said a grateful thanks and hoped they reached a hidey hole before the bullets flew.

There I was, living another contradiction. On one hand was the thrill of griz, wolf, moose and lion; on the other was Bud, Budweiser and bud. Two six packs a day and a toke or two. Five fingers clutched around a can, a one-handed wonder and a sad, s-a-d (stoned and drunk) man.

The early day forays into beauteous landscapes and wild critters ended with evening anti-government rants below his confederate flag: the introduction of grizzlies and wolves was a government plot to get people out of the woods; to make everyone buy meat at Costco. I couldn't have made that stuff up.

And it wasn't only Bud. Stoner paranoia extended to his good buddy, a gossip I called the Town Crier who felt it his duty to warn Bud I was after his money. Then there was the stoned spinster down the road who accused me of taking over his house. Was anyone straight? The answer was no, as I imagined a cartoon strip called s-a-d days at Happy's.

With doubts bearing down, one night Bud revealed past decades of break-ups, stalking, restraining orders, and hefty divorce pay-offs. Fifty shades of damned dark gray. Not my milieu. I wondered if all adventurous, edgy men were s-a-d. Did irreverence have to come with blackouts and face plants? I took a step back, craned my neck to see the proverbial forest for the trees. Bud was a portal to wild Montana and a sweet companion when sober, not to mention a fun cribbage competitor. I would stay a bit longer; the agent was in the throes of contacting a dozen top publishers. With partnership off the table I concentrated on communion with the wild and the intriguing culture of Happy's. Or as muse was fond of saying: *Everything's material.*

She tromped up the wooded hill as I rounded a dirt path. Her stout body paused as she cast me a wide smile. Another woman! A lively chat ensued: she and her farrier husband Doug were from Columbia Falls and had a cabin nearby. She was once a fire lookout and downplayed her background in anthropology in favor of a story about an herb that grew by a nearby lake. Glory be, an intelligent neighbor whose vibe was off the charts.

We gabbed on. She and Doug had owned their little piece of wilderness for decades. As much as I walked I'd never seen them. Their minimalist cabin was tucked deep into the forest; had no running water or electricity. Every few weeks they loaded up their small-farm menagerie – horses, goats, a dog and cat – and retreated to their Valhalla.

I'm just a backwoods herbalist using what grows here Ronny mused, as she handed me a jar of "Veronica's Montana Salve." Aha, she was an alchemist too. We promised to catch one another when she and Doug visited. They rode their horses over to look me up. I often opened the old wooden gate and sat on their cabin porch when they were gone. Soaked up the sun and a dose of Ronny vibe.

Fifteen miles in the opposite direction lived Trudi, the determined woman who transformed her acreage into a private wolf refuge. She was crazy-courageous to do what she did in the middle of Kill Club Land. Just as I was careful about who saw me get into the government truck with the State wolf biologist, she kept a low profile. She spent thousands of dollars to keep the howl alive. She owned my admiration.

I leaned on Trudi and Ronny for support. They knew one another but their paths didn't overlap. These two sisters had Hillary-hardened demeanors and supportive husbands. Like me, they knew how to use a gun. In keeping with the spirit of the 'hood I christened us the pussy posse. If one didn't play with the dark side one was doomed.

Twelve degrees. The silent woods were cloaked in a foot of new powder. While the urge to move south was strong, I answered the call to remain in this wild white world; to be here, shovel now. It had been a decade since I'd chosen winter in northern climes. One friend suggested we spend Thanksgiving in Death Valley and my spirit leapt. But this winter was not about ease or travel. It was about positioning financially: organizing photos, new book preparations, writing articles as I waited on the sure-fire book contract. I was content to track down a thrift store for winter boots, buy a new truck battery and drag deer blocks across the little river to watch the beauties feed. With all of the perversity in this outpost, I chose to mine dreams from deep dark forests and skies alight with the Milky Way. Awe was the other side of fear.

Bud and I had discovered an old growth larch sanctuary at autumn color peak. The remnants of an old hunting camp were strewn about, fun to photograph, to walk amidst the mystery. In the middle of the camp was a weathered two-shelf bookcase. A strange thing to find near a meat pole. Perhaps it once stored beans, knives and dish soap or held tablets from the likes of a Montana Thoreau. It captured my imagination and it wasn't going to sprout legs and walk several miles to my door.

By the time we drove the icy road to pick it up, the bookcase was frozen to the ground. We pried it loose and struggled across crusty snow to the truck, worth every awkward moment. Once thawed, I would adorn it with colored cloth and candles, beauty to coax the secreted stories of the woods – like the hushed great gray owl that perched on a larch limb and devoured a vole; the squeamish teenaged hunter who gutted a cow elk at creekside. The leaning yellow pine with bark that smelled of cinnamon.

Bud dried the case in his shop; several days later he reinforced it with stunning pine. It represented the kind of moment I like to remember of him. When all was said and done, I would leave it behind. It was too heavy a load for Perla.

Winter descent took many forms. The season's short days, Bud's nightly memory blackouts ... all for rich stories to be told and images to capture. Nature was the most luscious form of bondage, as I wrapped myself in protective ritual and moved between dazzle and dark. I lit fires and drummed at riverside. Every morning I sat cross-legged on the bed with a small tuning fork designed specifically for quartz crystals. I pinged the fork against the crystal and held it over my heart until the sound dissipated, about thirty seconds: *may my heart open to the love of the universe.* I repeated the ping four times: to my throat to *speak the unspeakable,* a lift to the third eye to *see the unseen.* I spiraled it above my crown *that I might connect to the cosmos.* And back to my heart. All to keep my energy steady; my vibration strong. I know it worked. No sooner did I stop and close my eyes than Hobo snug-purred between my breasts and nibbled my chin.

Many years ago a lover and I hiked into the wilderness. We approached a large fallen tree trunk. Without words we shed our clothes. I lay on my back as he covered me in kisses, our erotic communion one with azure sky and fiery sun. Apen leaves sparkled in the breeze as he moved inside, we, a pulsating oneness. Colors, textures, wet climactic groans.

We eventually sat up. I leaned on him as if drugged and waxed poetic on the sensuous scene when he suddenly asked: *What about me?* I stopped short. Such a strange question, as I realized he did not experience the same cosmic linkage as I.

Praise be women's precious bodies, built for sexual pleasure. Clitoral nerves wrap around our vaginas and reach 3.5 inches into the pelvis. We climax alone or with a partner irrespective of reproduction. Erotic pleasure is our birthright as orgasms deliver us to cosmic oneness. A-men. A-women. A-tonomy.

Winter's leaden days wore me down. The earliest sunset arrived two weeks earlier than the official start of winter; it felt like a personal affront. The sun hung in the sky like a 20-watt bulb. The landscape laid flat with no shadow. I responded with the only ammunition I could muster: bought a half gallon of heavy whipping cream at Costco.

I zapped my espresso with a teaspoon of cream, but how many teaspoons were in a half gallon? Freezing wouldn't work; it turned grainy. Fearing I'd overplayed my hand, I scoured the internet for whipped cream recipes but didn't find one that clicked. Then I remembered the red, 1950 first-edition *Betty Crocker's Picture Cook Book* that Aunt Clara had given me when I was first married. I was nineteen. She'd also given me a Stanley's kitchen broom. It was Iowa, after all. At least I didn't get a Jell-O mold.

In those tattered, taped, butter-smudged pages was a recipe for a chocolate cream pie, fit for any kitchen table. I made it my own: dark chocolate powder instead of squares or chips; whipping cream instead of milk; a half cup of espresso and a pinch of red chile powder. I cooked up the cauldron of midnight-dark pudding. It was thick and rich, unlike any concoction I had ever tasted. Once cool, I poured it into my flakey pastry shell and covered it with high peaks of whipped cream. I cut the first two pieces and Bud and I drove down the snow-packed path to deliver them to Ronny and Doug.

They met us at the door in shock – couldn't believe their eyes seeing headlights in the night, pie at their door. A scream of delight broke the silence of the woods. *It's Doug's favorite!* cried Ronny. Back home, alone by the fire, I served up a slice … slowly savored the creamy dark. Swallowed solstice.

I was grinding the morning coffee beans when movement caught my eye. About thirty yards outside the sliding door, across the little river, was a bobcat. She sniffed grasses and alder thickets, in no obvious hurry. I glassed her striped body. She was small with sharp edges. She proceeded to the mineral block, glanced at me and disappeared into the brush.

I wasn't looking for a sign but had just received one. I was a Tiger by the Chinese calendar. I'd had potent encounters with mountain lions and the jaguar meeting in Tikal. Now I moved from big cats to small, from thick, mighty tails to minute bobs. My inquiry commenced.

Bobcats were solitary prowlers of the dawn and dusk, immersed in a silent, secretive world. Not unlike crepuscular me, I mused. They prowled through river bottoms; I prowled, pen in hand, through thickets of imagination. Bobcats were stealth hunters with keen senses. They had an uncanny ability to blend in and survive in their environment. Perhaps too true where I was concerned.

The little cats averaged two to four feet long, fifteen inches tall and twenty-five pounds. The bobcat was my competition when it came to spotting a snowshoe hare. The white wonders were the bob's preferred diet. Thus far I'd seen many tracks but not the hare. I longed to spot one.

I read on. The bobcat was associated with wind in mythology and paired with coyote. Coyote was disorder, bobcat was order. My short-tailed friend was the cosmological protector of Venus, Goddess of love, my ruling planet. In my ancestors' Norse mythology, bobcat was associated with Freya, Goddess of love, beauty and destiny, who rode a chariot pulled by two cats (to whom Hobo claimed to be a direct descendant.)

Lynx Rufus. Lynx, from the word for light. So named for gleaming eyes; the ability to see in the dark. A bobcat traveled up to seven miles a day and had a range of one hundred square miles. I'd be lucky to see her again. I committed her qualities to memory: stealth, power, camouflage and clairaudience – hearing sounds and voices not audible to most. I wondered if she heard trees speak.

I mentioned bobcat's visitation to Bud.

That's a $300 bill! he said.

This one was too small I stammered.

Could be more than that … the small ones have the best coats.

Don't you ***dare*** *tell a soul.*

He promised silence. He's wasn't a trapper but there were plenty around, including the Town Crier. I ceased to tell Bud when I spotted wildlife.

Carole arrived from Kaslo; she had an uncanny way of showing up when she sensed I was in a tough spot. She knew my propensity for deal-making. With money dwindling, no book contract and Bud's beer-propelled tirades, this was an increasingly costly deal. She wanted to check it out. We three broke the ice with a cross-country ski to a small mountain lake. We had the place to ourselves; found boulders and logs, sat, picnicked and worshipped the sun. Up was a slog, down was screaming, laughing fun with the speed of a bobsled run, plowing into drifts to slow our speed. The hot tub never felt better. We were off to a good start.

The next day was Valentine's Day. Hearts, flowers and candy to most, I celebrated its ancient meaning. Once called Lupercalia, it was the olden celebration of sexual heat. Lupercalia was named after Lupa, the wolf, the aged symbol of the instinct to breed. I'd noticed their fist-sized tracks in the snow for weeks, dotted with urine scent marks and digs. Every wolf sign excited me. My initial wait-and-see mode had morphed into unrelenting support of the wolves. Studies showed that the deer and elk population drops were due to weather; lions took more elk than wolves.

The three of us drove the gravel roads to Lost Prairie, an expansive meadowland flanked by forests and lakes. We walked on snow-covered ice to a small island; frozen steps across a white world. The only other humans were a couple of ice fishermen in lawn chairs a half mile away, augers at their sides. I stepped off the bank into a half foot of snow and mapped out a ten foot heart with my footsteps – a valentine to the wild. And then they showed up.

We'd driven several miles beyond the snow heart when we spotted him running across a field. Wolf! *Stop!* I jumped out and ran up the road for a closer look. Awestruck at his size and grace, we watched as he strode confidently out of sight. I turned back to the truck and there stood two, side-by-side. As Carole, Bud and I had looked one way, these had crossed behind us. I walked toward them. One fled, one stayed. Our eyes locked as we shared our curiosity for one another. I moved closer; she turned and slipped into the thick-pined hill.

It was hard to crawl back into the truck. The energy was electric. Carole and I were euphoric as Bud complained he had no gun to shoot them. No one got a shot off that day. I was too enraptured to put the viewfinder to my eye.

That night we played cribbage and darts until Bud staggered off to bed. Carole and I returned to the thrill of the wolves when my phone rang with the voice of my friend John from Taos. I told him about the wolves; the smoke-a pack-a-day mentality. *Forest farming elk is big business.* He wasn't one to mince words. We talked about his struggle to pen his latest book. *It's hard to write a book now* he said. *Very hard.* He was seventy-two. Had bone spurs that hurt when he walked. His daily hike up Taos's Divisidero was more and more a challenge.

Carole. John. Our paths dated back to my solo cabin days in the San Luis Valley. What were the chances of two great loves and me meeting at the confluence of three wolves and Lupercalia? Urine and blood-tinted snow. A forest full of lust. A low, lonely howl seeped through bedroom walls. Lest (lust) you forget me, he implied. Not a chance.

Carole departed the next morning. She encouraged me to leave soon, but seeing the wolves, she understood my choice. *Don't dawdle* she said.

It was a late start; an indecisive morn. I'd read of an irruption of Snowy Owls two hours south at the end of Flathead Lake. I had planned to nail the specific location but got distracted by a Pileated Woodpecker who swooped by my head. The first one I'd ever seen was weaving between fence posts in California's wine country, drunk on fermented grapes. I considered the Pileated a sure sign of a magical morning, perfect for Snowy Owls. Bud was game.

We didn't spot one Arctic ghost as we passed through Polsen and south onto plains that resembled their barren tundra home. I spotted a car ahead on an otherwise empty gravel road. *Catch up, it's a birder and he'll know where the owls are.* Bud cast me his too familiar Miss-Know-It-All look. I was undaunted. I recognized my ilk. The kind man had just spotted seven Snowy Owls and gave directions. Back we went to town.

We turned onto a side street and there they were, perched on snow-blotched rooftops with a 360 degree view that included Flathead

Lake to the north and hunting fields below. Puffy, fluffy ghost-white sentinels. I counted twelve as we drove around the neighborhood. We parked and walked through snow for another view; a photographic angle to portray their regal beauty and presence.

I'd never seen a Snowy Owl. Irruptions were normal every few years, when nomadic groups departed their Arctic home in winter and traveled further south than normal. During the last irruption to Polson they wintered a mile away, laying claim to fence posts and old farm machinery. Now the solitary ones hung out on housetops as if they were the most sociable creatures alive. Irruptions were usually regional, but this year thousands of owls had come south from coast to coast. Seattle. Kansas. The Ohio River Valley. Boston. Denver International Airport.

The Snowy diet is 90% lemmings; when food supply dwindled in their circumpolar home they moved south in winter. But these diurnal birds did not look starved or stressed. I felt they'd come to dazzle with pure white awakening. A female defending her chicks would launch at a predator from a half mile away at twenty-five mph. With stealth bomber acumen, she tore through cotton layers, down jackets and flesh with ease. No wonder the fierce Oglala warriors wore caps of these birds' powerful feathers into battle.

Yes, the Snowy Owls had arrived in unprecedented numbers. They lifted off from melting ice caps to land on rooftops that we might marvel; give thought to a planet out of kilter. What would it take to open hearts and minds and turn the world around? Late starts *could* reap results.

On the first day of spring I dreamed I killed myself with a .22 pistol. I shot once into my mouth and nothing happened so I did it again. I didn't feel abnormal but I knew I hadn't missed twice. I went into the hallway and told Carole. She sat with me as I died, holding my hand. *I'm sorry* I said. *Tell Hope I love her*. She nodded yes and put cotton gauze into my mouth. I took it out: *Not yet, I have more to say.*

I laughed. Dreams! I scribbled down the words *Wild Road Home*, a book I'd yet to write.

I saw a mink at sunset as we readied to leave for a party. I was tempted to skip the soiree in favor of river time but looked forward to meeting the woman who owned the lakeside home. By then I'd met three women, not nearly enough, as I held off membership in the camo crockpot club.

The party started out fun. Lively conversation and friendly spirits. Energy turned, however, when the guys began to stumble around drunk with loaded guns. Not my scene. I wanted to leave and Bud agreed, then changed his mind in favor of *one more for the road.* I planned to drive but grew tired of waiting. I told him I'd meet him up the road and began to walk on the ebony starlit night. I figured he'd be along soon. He wasn't.

I waited for him when I reached the highway. When he didn't show up, I turned down the highway and kept walking. I hadn't gone far when he roared up behind, swerved so close I jumped; scared the bejezus of out me.

Get in he ordered. Not on your life.

Let me drive. I'm not going to ride with a drunk.

Get in! I backed away.

Two cars pulled over on the highway, one with women and one with men. Both drivers got out and ran toward us. Bud drove off. *Are you okay?* they asked. I shook with fear and disbelief. They had no idea where I lived but both offered me a ride. I chose the van with the two women. I climbed in the back with their children; calmed down amidst their play. They were going home to Kalispell from a craft fair in Libby. To take me home they had to turn around. Bless their hearts.

Thanks for stopping I said, embarrassed and shocked at what had unfolded.

Don't say another word. My two sisters were killed by a drunk driver. She cast a caring glance in the rearview mirror and steered me toward home.

I took refuge in Perla as Bud's hateful rants avalanched through the dark. No one escaped his verbal aim – women, Jews, people of color, wolves, my friends. Gun and phone within reach, I trembled on my bed. The *SNAPS!* were too many to count. Taped to my door the next morning was a note that read "You're fired!!!"

I gathered courage, stepped down Perla's stairs and walked toward the house. It was reckoning time. He knew it too – his door was locked. I let myself in with the hidden key; we met at the couch. After several minutes, Bud spoke first.

You embarrassed me when you started walking. Your antics could have gotten me a DUI.

Did he hear his own words? My *antics*?

He didn't remember swerving, almost hitting me and ordering me into the car. Didn't recall driving home or the tirade that followed.

You could have killed someone. Doesn't it bother you that you don't remember what you did?

Nope.

I took a breath and struggled to stay calm.

You know, you have the time, you have the money, how about you go into treatment. If you want, I'll stay longer and take care of things here.

I bet you would.

It was time to visit the old-growth ponderosa I had spotted months earlier. Bud had kept walking the day I stopped and sat at her base; stared into her twisted, massive limbs. It took the gravity of the drunk episode to get me back to her. The drive was lengthy; gravel and tight curves kept it slow. I parked at a dead-end road and hiked up the mountainside past abandoned logging camps. I rounded a corner and saw her in the distance. Almost there.

I stepped into a narrow, nondescript creek bed and sank. One leg, up to my ankle. Then further, to the shin. Up to the knee. Teak stared from the other side as my panicked mind searched for options. One leg was free, but the more I tried to extract myself, the deeper I sank. I stopped struggling and took a deep breath. I leaned at the waist to change the center of gravity, took another breath and, ever so slowly, out-muscled the suction and pulled my leg free.

I crawled onto the bank; sat still as death to calm frayed nerves. I could have been in there forever. I rose and made my way to the tree; planted a hi-glad-to-be-alive kiss against her fire-scarred bark.

Quicksand. Remember that, Christina, as you decide to stay or go.

Quicksand. I recalled numerous hikes up southwest washes when I had followed deer tracks between pockets of morass. They knew. They sensed. This, on the other hand, was a quagmire pit. I lay beneath her branches, mud-caked leg and all, and let the pent-up emotion of weeks past stream out.

Why hadn't I hitched up Perla and driven away? Against all rational thought, my feelings told me it wasn't time yet. The suicide dream said I had more to say; more to glean. Subconscious threads kept me in place, as if the soul were preparing me for some future time. This initiation was as relevant as the jaguar's.

Roots run deep; connections are invisible.

Yes.

Not all survive. Some things are so authentic they kill you.

I gazed skyward through her branches. The energy from her roots penetrated my butt and traveled up my back, a full-body dizzying charge. I had met the jaguar and emerged with my name. Now, as then, faith put me here.

I can do this. I will not be sixty sexy solo and stuck.

That night I dreamed I told off my mother, something I'd never done in real life. I had long gone silent in the face of her sarcasm and found love in the company of aunts. I never understood sarcasm. Children don't. I was very different from the older sister and brother who comprised the offspring who were planned. Born ten years after my older sister, I reckon I put a damper on her freedom dreams.

Ours had been a rocky road punctuated with stultifying events, like the morning she and I leaned supine into the webbing of our chaise lawn chairs. I had recently returned from my freshman year at college. I could hardly contain myself; excited to share classes and roommate escapades.

Do you want to know about my year? She glanced at me, looked away, and in a glib voice of finality said *No.*

Now this dream. What forces gathered beneath the ground, tangled the roots of my family tree? I flashed back to Carole's Tarot reading warning me of karmic knots; wondered if Tam and Bud were some kind of preparation.

I would stay the course. Writing was my service. My purpose. I was a purveyor of wild places and the spirits that held sway over souls. Some drank from bottles, I drank from the well of words. Just how far I would go was yet to be seen as the road spiraled toward the Mothers – my biological flesh and planet home.

Teak and I walked every day. I watched rapt as a moose mother and calf fed in a willow-clad bog. A fat, hefty black bear boar rested in a huckleberry patch. Elk lowered their heads and drank from Banana Lake. Two wily wolves disappeared as I rounded a hilltop. All of this, twenty minutes from Perla's door.

I relished the feel of fine hairs erect on my neck, my breath taken, brain catapulted into fear-fight-flight mode. My participation in the food chain validated my existence. Heart to wild heart, I *was* nature. Never more true than when Mama Moose stepped out of the Fisher River into the yard with her day old calf.They were so close, the newborn so vulnerable! I watched through the window as they moved closer. The babe intrigued by every tree and blade of grass.

I slowly opened the door and moved onto the deck, alert for signs of Mom's discomfort. I'd heard the enraged Mama moose stories – tales of a lightning fast charge, stomp and death. This mom, however, relayed calm.

I stepped off the deck into the grass, ten yards away, as she and babe allowed me into their world. Babe sniffed flowers, watched birds, wobbled up to a plastic green chair and stretched to lick. I photographed and talked to them, mom with one eye on me, one on her newborn. They eventually crossed the yard, stepped off the bank and returned to the river. Babe positioned between mom's legs, they disappeared upstream.

Nine months had passed since the agent declared me a brand and foretold a book contract and movie options. I'd had no offers and plenty of thoughtful rejections. My savings dwindled as book dreams crumbled. A general anxiety overtook me as I felt the pressure of migration. I needed the book and I needed it now. *Publish it yourself* said Bud. Friends joined the refrain.

I researched self-publishing online and talked with professionals in the field. Excitement overcame desperation as I convinced myself that yes, I could do it. Self-publishing was no longer second class vanity, it was indie. I checked with my agent who agreed with my choice. Once she secured the book contract I would transfer the intellectual rights to the publisher. I forged ahead. I'd waited nine months. It was time to birth this baby.

Six stress-fueled weeks and six hundred dollars later, the book proof arrived at the door via UPS. I tore back the cardboard and squealed with joy. *Drive Me Wild: A Western Odyssey* was in my hands. The back cover blurbs of praise brought tears; the red font on the front was dead-on right. There I was, sitting Zen-like on a rock in Avalanche Lake, peering into distant peaks, beckoning readers to join me in my odyssey.

The book. Five years of my life. I pushed the proof in front of Bud. He made a snide comment about my ass at Avalanche Lake and ordered a hundred copies. That night I dreamed I was on the Sonoran Desert. I walked a trail alone, glassing the mountains. I spied a lion moving through saguaro. She suddenly rose onto her hind legs and began swatting at birds. Pure power delight.

I sprayed a quick burst of Chanel N°5 the air and ducked under the aromatic haze. Olfactory, tingly muse-mist. She adored it. My robe-covered flesh chilled as I filled the feeder with sunflower seeds; said good morning to Pine Siskin, Evening Grosbeak, Red-breasted Nuthatch, Mountain and Black-capped Chickadees and Cassin's Finch. My morning symphony, movement in Awe-Major.

Chanel and I went way back. My first boyfriend gave me a bottle for high school graduation. It was tucked under a bouquet of long-stemmed red roses. Decades later that bottle was still on my bedside altar. A few years back, a friend from Paris brought me some spray cologne and a book on Luxembourg Gardens. Now I emailed friend Joe to pick up a bottle in the duty free store. If convenient. He did. Perfume, not cologne. *Congratulations on your book!*

Everything I bought was fragrance free... detergent, deodorant, toilet paper, tissue. Yet there I was, seducing the muse with Chanel N°5. Sometimes sage and sweet grass didn't cut it.

One foot in the Montana wild, one foot aimed south. Book promotion and website updates ruled my life as I prepared Perla for departure. Seeking solace, I made for the deep woods back roads. I rolled slowly around deep ruts and holes when something moved about twenty feet in front of the tires. Waddle waddle went the low-slung body. She turned her head to reveal that unmistakable black and white striped face. You cannot come across badger medicine and pretend it didn't happen.

She looked in my direction and waddled away. Then she turned back! She pointed her nose at me and returned to the spot where she'd rolled in the dirt. She eventually turned her dusty fur away and disappeared southward into the forest. I grabbed my camera but she was gone as could be. That was fine. Communion came first.

Badger. Earth energy didn't get any stronger. They burrowed faster through the planet than any other creature. Thus, they are a birth talisman for Natives, to assist a newborn child through the dark birth canal. Badgers are bold, ferocious and unyielding, solitary and highly aggressive when threatened. Badger people need solitary space and major down time.

Mostly, however, badgers represent nose-to-the-grindstone work ethic. They encapsulate dig-in focus and energy. That night I asked my dreams for insight on my timely encounter. I watched myself work furiously, like a badger, on my website and posting the button that said "BUY now."

Badgers were also an omen for prosperity through effort. I disengaged from my agent as I grasped the advantages of keeping control of my intellectual property. Going indie suited me.

Like Tam before him, guy-guide Bud had delivered me into wild places I would otherwise never have touched. Wolf. Black bear. Badger. Bobcat. Bighorn Sheep. Griz. Snowy Owl. Mink. Tundra Swan. Harlequin Duck. Thousands of migrating ladybugs. Short-eared Owl. Mother and baby moose. Drumming and campfires along the river. I recalled the blustery day we gazed down from a mountain perch upon a lynx trolling a streambed through thick snow.

I had participated in field work with a Montana wolf biologist and a Snowy Owl expert. I had talked to a grizzly biologist and hiked mountains with the Yaak environmental group intent on preserving griz habitat. Their devotion to science on behalf of the wild was exemplary. But I was not content with data collection and formal study. My soul sought to join with that mother moose.

I dug ballsy-competent men for their capacity to exist on the edge. Alas, Bud's alcoholism, like Tam's, was part of that. This time it had delivered me to the confluence of a confederate flag and sacred feminine principle, where all land was the Holy Land. I had garnered all the insights I needed; it was time to hit the wild road. Beyond the quicksand. Home.

It was my final night. Packing complete, I made my solitary way to the hot tub, pushed the cover aside and lowered myself into the water. A Great Horned Owl hoot erupted across the river, his stately silhouette in the top of the pine. I sank into the tub until I barely saw him over the cover. Then I gently scratched my fingernail across the vinyl. Could they really hear as well as I had read? He was fifty yards away, across the babbling river.

The owl perked up, spread his wings and launched in split-second response. He soared over my head within inches and continued into darkness. Whoo whoo hoo hoo … Whoo stays, whoo goes?

Everyone, eventually.

Thank you on my lips, I slipped under the amniotic water.

Teak waited patiently in Blue. Hobo cast an inquisitive look through the window of Perla, downright annoyed that I'd fit him with a harness. Bud helped lift the hitch into the receiver. It was early in the morning, before Budweiser time, so both his hands were free.

Good to go. He shyly looked my way. Relief. Love. Gloom. Ire. Gratitude. A crazy range of emotions wrapped themselves in our short shallow hug.

It's been a slice he said.

His words, eerily reminiscent, of someone.

Montana Ponderosa Pine, quicksand witness.

Part Three

The Wild Yes

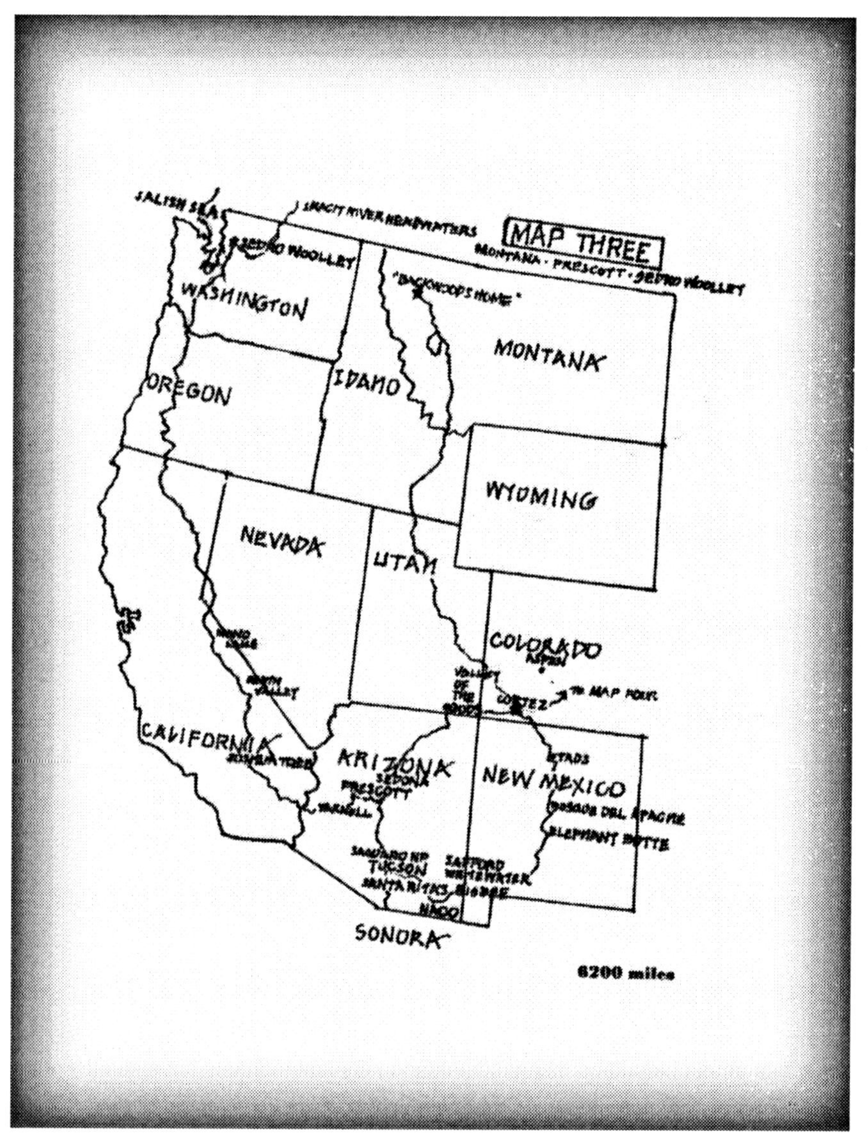

MAP THREE
MONTANA · PRESCOTT · SEDRO WOOLLEY
SALISH SEA
SKAGIT RIVER HEADWATERS
SEDRO WOOLLEY
WASHINGTON
OREGON
IDAHO
MONTANA
WYOMING
NEVADA
UTAH
COLORADO
CORTEZ
CALIFORNIA
ARIZONA
SEDONA
PRESCOTT
TUCSON
NEW MEXICO
ELEPHANT BUTTE
SONORA
6200 miles

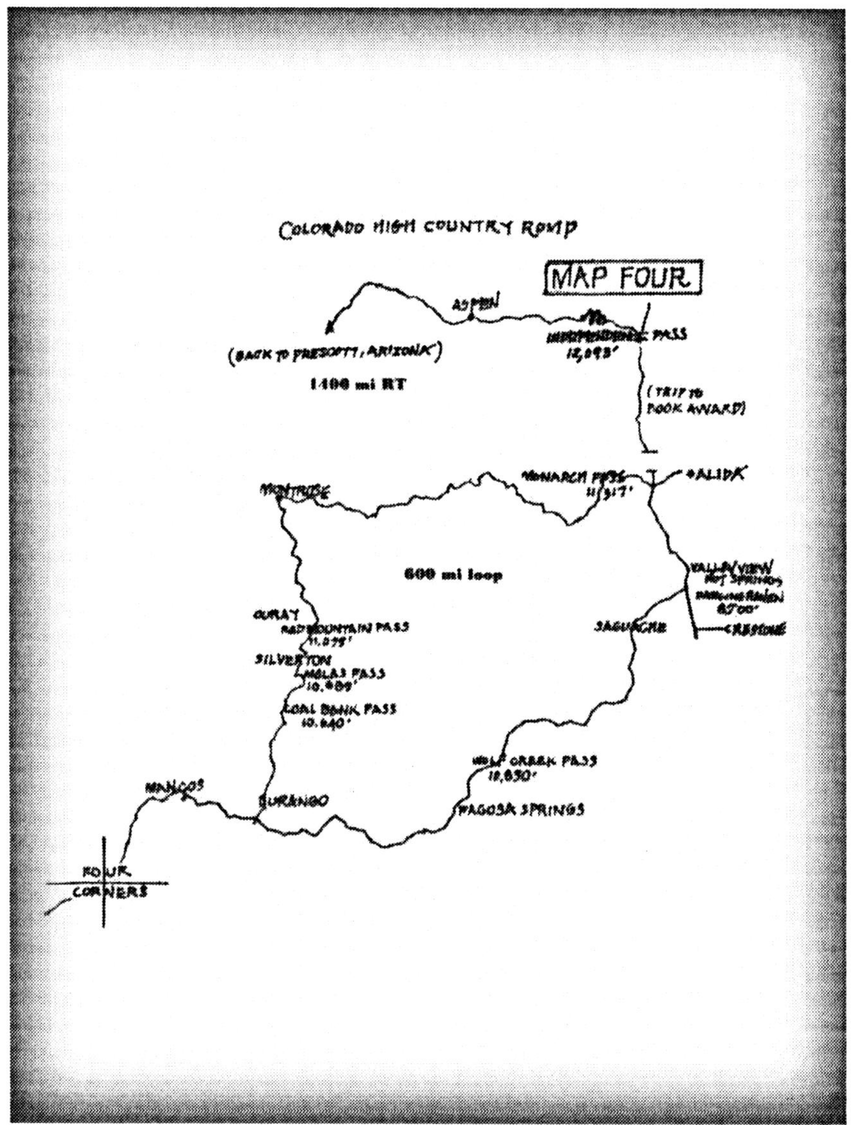
COLORADO HIGH COUNTRY ROMP
MAP FOUR
ASPEN
PASS
(BACK TO PRESCOTT, ARIZONA)
1400 mi RT
(TRIP TO BOOK AWARD)
MONARCH PASS
MONTROSE
600 mi loop
OURAY
SILVERTON
COAL BANK PASS
10,640'
SAGUACHE
PAGOSA SPRINGS
DURANGO
MANCOS
FOUR CORNERS

The steel frame towered above as I stood in front of the swings. There were six. Three groups of two on the elementary school playground. They dropped down on chains sporting black rubber seats. I liked the one on the far right. It was lower than the rest and my bare feet touched the ground.

I wiggled my eight-year-old butt onto the seat, clenched the chain and pushed off. Leaning back, pushing forward, I pumped the swing into a pendulum arc. Sometimes I jumped out at this point. Sailing through the air, I landed and ran forward several steps. But if I didn't jump, I stood up. Bent my legs, pumped and continued the climb.

I wanted to swing as high as the top of the bar. Into heaven. I imagined going completely over, cartoon-like, in a daring circle. But just when I reached the apex the chains went slack, and for a split second I free fell until the chain tightened with a thrill-scary jerk.

Alone in my joy, I was fearless.

I pulled out of Bud's lane on November 13, a couple weeks after my 62nd birthday. Bud had gifted me with a set of new tires. I got the hint. My month-long Montana book tour complete, it was a timely exit on the heels of Obama's re-election. I was silent in my glee as the first black president spawned a new round of backwoods tirades.

I drove east on the heels of a new moon eclipse, toward Costco in Kalispell. There was a smart phone inside with my name on it. My first. The young sales guy was sweet and patient with Luddite-woman. He set me up and gave me a quickie Droid intro as I asked him if the phone had a vibrator app. His professional demeanor collapsed into laughter. He handed me a card at the end of his tutorial. He said he wasn't always available at Costco but invited me to call him from the road if I had questions. *I'd like to have a life like yours* he said. *Drive Me Wild* I smiled and handed him my card. *Read all about it!*

I returned to the truck as daylight waned, did my walk-around check and saw trouble. The electrical cord that ran from Perla and plugged into the back of the truck had loosened, dragged on the asphalt and worn through to the wires. Eeee, damn. I had no trailer turn signals or running lights, good for a ticket or worse, an accident. I high-tailed it to my planned stay with Ronny and Doug in Columbia Falls, signaling with my arm out the window. A dark half hour later I pulled into their farm, one frazzled puppy, and fell into their hugs.

Ronny flipped us some whole grain pancakes in the morning while Doug spliced the electrical cord together and wound it up tight with black electrical tape. With teary thanks and goodbyes, I headed south. I had no ultimate destination in mind. The road had taught me that most plans got in the way of life.

Perla shadowed behind, running lights aglow, as we traced the east side of Flathead Lake to Polson. The owls were long gone but my eyes still glimpsed those rooftops. Habits die hard. Once I had a wild encounter I didn't forget the location. A bear by a certain tree. A steep sunny ridge with lazing pumas. A burrowing owl perched on a prairie dog hole.

Ah, Montana. I will miss you. Tears welled and just like that, the voice in my head took a vindictive turn. *What the hell are you doing?* My unplanned world turned tenuous. Autonomous woman gave way to trailer trash. My stomach turned. *Steady, Womad.* I knew what this was. It was the letdown of a love that never materialized; the loneliness of choosing purpose. I let the feelings rise and fall. The miles passed as resolve returned. *A committed relationship will appear, but it won't be a mate attached at the hip or a white picket fence.* Hm, yes.

The requisites were shifting. That little tête-à-tête out of the way, I smiled at my book on the passenger seat.

I was closing in on Butte when I saw the sign for Fairmont Hot Springs, two miles off the highway. Why not? The sun was over the yardarm and I needed a place to park for the night. I passed a snowed-in, closed campground at the outskirts of the small town. A half mile later was the resort hot springs. Emphasis on resort. It was $150 a night for a room, and no, I couldn't stay in their empty overflow parking lot.

Back to the closed campground I went. There was one woman camper in the otherwise deserted place. *You alone, too?* she asked. I love it when that happens. *Park anywhere. Power's on.* The rest of her group was up the road but, like me, she didn't like motels and preferred her own food. I put Blue in 4WD and barreled into a space through six inches of crusty snow.

Site secured and tracks made to ensure an easy return, I hurried back to the hot springs. The daily senior rate was $4.75. I liked sixty-two more and more; that is, until the clerk didn't ask my age. Come on, humor me.

The water was silky-warm sublime – large indoor and steamy outdoor pools. Lifeguards dressed for winter temps in boots, hats and parkas. I breast stroked under the Milky Way as a four-story water slide at the far end of the pool winked at my soul. The duel went something like this: *C'mon, Christina. Not on your life. Ah c'mon. No way. WAY.* Alone in the pool, I climbed four levels of stairs and stared into the tube, nothing short of a birth canal.

I paused, stepped inside with a gulp and slid quickly into several tight turns. Water and steepness pushed me onto the sides as I gained scary-exhilarating speed, tipping and swishing like an out-of-whack pendulum. I entered a straightaway, saw light and SPLASH. I screamed into the steam, touched bottom and hopped up and down in a happy dance. I took a deep breath and pushed off into a back float; spied the new crescent moon overhead and started to shake. *Let everything happen to you: beauty and terror. Just keep going. No feeling is final,* wrote Rilke. Wildlife, wildscape, wildman. Montana wouldn't let go of me.

I had asked Bud if he wanted me to stay while he sought treatment. He said he'd been through counseling's *why-do-you-hate-yourself* regimen.

The better question would have been *Why so … sad?*

Both he and Tam had experienced traumatic moments of loss; unchecked grief that turned into venom. *Why so sad?* – the universal question. Sadness was the bedrock of emotional time.

My personal inquisition had taken sundry forms. At the nethermost was Earth and Her wild – the innocent, sentient beings swept toward extinction by humans who lost their way. While our species acknowledged our own consciousness it denied the planet's and other life forms. If not mended, this separation would be our undoing.

I made my arduous way through Salt Lake City and headed up the infamous climb toward Price. Yes, the one that almost did me in on that first solo womad day. I gassed up and began the descent toward Moab and desert starkness. I saw my first prairie dog in months, standing on hind legs along the road. A badger turned her striped head and met my eyes as I passed a barren field. I'd only seen two in my life before Montana, now I'd seen two in as many weeks. *Keep-digging, Christina.*

I pulled into the Arches Visitor's Center to pick up a coveted National Parks card: ten bucks and free entrance until I die. Half-price camping, too. I'd long wanted to overnight at Arches. The campground was small, simple and had vacancies. Up the steep cliffside I drove into sandstone and sky, queen of the world.

Camping spot secured, I stepped into sundown. Teak and Hobo followed as I inhaled the endless view. No juniper branch moved. No grass frond swayed. All was succulent stillness. And then, the cra-aaack of a raven. Before I knew it, a conspiracy of eight flocked above Hobo, dive-bombing his position. He ducked, I opened Perla's door and he leapt inside as his attackers glided away, their wingbeats like finger nails across silk.

Your thick tree cover is gone, eh, Hobo?

He wasn't amused as his eyes scanned the sky.

Perla filled with light as I watched the sun lift off the horizon for the first time in over a year, no longer hemmed in by trees. Vistas delivered brilliant bursts of pale yellow and distant rock silhouettes. I'd only planned on one night but I was nowhere near ready to depart. I tracked down the campground host, introduced myself, gave her an autographed book and paid for another night. I'd been to Arches many times. I'd hiked ruddy-red sandstone to Delicate Arch; stood before etched petroglyphs and wandered speechless in towering rock canyons. This time I would hike the smaller arches away from the day-visit crowds that would inundate the park by noon.

Four days beyond Montana, mojo intact, I called in an order of eggplant parmesan to Pasta Jay's in Moab. I picked up the garlic-laden sack and sped twenty miles south to Wilson Arch pullout; parked where I could feast and take in the scene. First bite into the gooey garlic bread a semi pulled up next to me and blocked my view. WTF? I closed the container, pushed the food aside and pulled forward.

Settled again, I was winding pasta around my fork when a short woman in fine jeans and a casual jacket walked up. She looked like she had stepped out of a Tupperware party. She sweetly asked if I'd like my picture taken with the Arch. I swallowed and glanced back over my shoulder. There weren't any cars. I asked if the truck was hers. Her eyes twinkled yes. So much for stereotypes.

She apologized for blocking my view and described a nerve-wracking trip from Seattle; how a guy in a little pickup had changed lanes and blocked traffic so she could maneuver through the turn lanes. I liked this gutsy woman. She was fascinated by my life on the road. I took her picture and she took mine as we reckoned we were two lucky women. We hugged goodbye, she mounted her rig and headed south toward Monticello. I would follow her route after I heated my food and finished my feast. I was an easy day's drive from where my quest had begun.

Go wake up your luck! – Persian proverb. My delayed eggplant parm was perfect.

I pulled into Cortez Lynn's in serious girlfriend deficit. I cranked up *Stop Making Sense,* jumped from the truck and we danced a boisterous hello in the driveway. Parking Perla would wait as we proceeded to the farmhouse kitchen, concocted gin and tonics and plopped down on the back porch. Sisterhood. We lit our ritual cigars and let the mood turn pensive as the sun set on the Mesa Verde plateau. Home of sprawling Anasazi cliff dwellings and prowling pumas, it was also the place of many recent memories. I lifted my glass to the familiar landscape that encompassed red-rock canyons splattered with potsherds. Not to mention one ex-husband and a spotted cat.

I'd no more finished off-loading and repacking, hoping to sit still for a few days, when I received an offer to housesit in Taos. Taos, where Grandmother Tree had once charged me to grow my hair long and take to the unknown road. The invitation was auspicious. Eight years, and thousands of miles beyond that original exhortation, spirit conspired to bring me back.

I said yes as my first social security check ker-chinged into my bank account. The day before departure I entered *Drive Me Wild* into the competition for the Colorado Book Award.

Ranchos de Taos in the winter – it was not my normal toasty Arizona or a tide-sculpted Mexico beach, yet there I was in my friend's studio while he traveled to Belgium to pursue a new love. Teak and Hobo settled into the curved metal shed-made-house on the edge of pastureland. They had lots of room to wander and clucking hens to keep them entertained.

Two days in I slogged through snow and slush to the Ranchos post office. The line of people bearing Christmas packages was long. *Just my luck, I only want to buy one stamp* I uttered. *Just one stamp?* asked a woman in front of me. I looked into the eyes of a friend I hadn't seen in a decade. Suzanne laughed: *Have I got a stamp for YOU!* as she planted a big kiss on my cheek. Then she handed me a stamp.

The next morning I drove east into a Sangre de Cristo canyon, excited, yet on edge. What if I didn't remember how to find her? It had been eight years since my last meeting with Grandmother Tree. Worry subsided as I remembered the turnoff. I geared Blue into 4WD and started up the snowy gravel. The road narrowed into a steep climb as shoulders disappeared. No worries now, the dead-end loop was in sight. The parking pullout had a foot of untracked snow.

I wished I'd brought snowshoes. My slow going became a walking meditation; a proper preparation to meet the Grand Dame of the forest. Apprehension and excitement grew as I wondered what I'd find. Had She been cut down? Had fire taken Her? I rounded the final snowy bend to view a forest intact. There She towered, in the middle of aspen, oak, fir and ponderosa.

I leaned into Her ruddy bark and inhaled the butterscotch scent. The smell of home. I laid my vest on the ground under Her thick boughs and took a seat. A Red-tailed hawk soared high. Snow fell with soft ker-plunks from the branches of nearby pines. A blissful hour passed before calm gave way to a nervous tic in my eye. *Here it comes.* There was no escaping the avalanche of recollections, from Alaska's Siren song to Montana's feral rumble.

You had your butt kicked, didn't you?

I managed a faint smile.

Ya. O ya.

I clenched snow as nuthatch clowns climbed upside down on tree trunks.

There are no wrong turns, Christina.

My tongue licked tears.

No wrong turns I muttered, as a parade of emotions commenced.

Doubt. Fear. Angst. Utter exhaustion.

Another hour passed. Raven flyovers punctuated the azure sky.

No wrong turns, that's right. Resolve eked back. Look what I'd done! I'd garnered the courage to quest. The words took hold, lifting my spirit, not so, however, my butt, which I suddenly realized was numb. Damp and cold had caught up with me. I reached for a seashell and a grouse feather in the pack. Treasures from my journey. I left them at the base of Her trunk and sprinkled some tobacco. I kissed Her bark and turned to go.

Take time to unfold your divinity She said.

I swallowed hard.

Christina, the quicksand is behind you.

How did She …? Never mind.

I took a circuitous route to the truck, through deep snow on the backside; cast a holy hello to the Pueblo's sacred mountain. *Unfold my divinity* I mumbled, a mantra to movement as gravity carried me downhill. My boots soaking wet, I followed my footsteps through snow to the truck. I turned up the heater and headed toward town with one stop to go. My spirit brimmed full but an empty stomach wailed; I ordered up the first green chile cheeseburger I could find.

That night I settled in with Hobo and Teak, went on the internet and ordered a new camera. A Lumix with a 24-600mm zoom, considered a flagship for low-light shoots. My nocturnal Bobcat friend would be proud.

The day before Grandmother Tree declared life had *kicked my butt,* I'd written *I'd almost sunk my ship,* referring to Montana. A popular astrologer remarked that *2012 rocked your boat and you're still afloat.* There was no mistaking I'd survived an initiation. Book signings, indie classes and radio shows blossomed from Santa Fe to Salida. I stopped dating and set my sites on photographing the bighorn sheep that frequented a nearby canyon. There was no better teacher for how to let go than nature and her seasonal changes.

The studio housesit space was sparsely furnished. I needed more than an office chair to sit in the toasty, radiant-heated living room. I purchased a love seat at a thrift store and set up my music stand;

strummed my gee-tar as the coldest temps in years descended on Taos. The water froze at eighteen below. Hobo and Teak hunkered down on the couch as empty Perla stood abandoned in the driveway. I still hadn't figured out how to gracefully come down the ladder from the loft at 3:00 a.m. to pee. The solution, I guessed, was to forego chamomile tea before my head hit the pillow.

No place vied with the mystical mix of Taos in December. The spirit-bending aroma of piñon wood smoke sent the brain far afield as shadow flames danced inside brown paper bags called *farolitos*. Black and white magpies cavorted en masse on *latilla* fences as if to taunt long shadows. Crystal snowflakes drifted from night's ebony sky and lined soft adobe ridgelines. Hope visited from Oregon for solstice, girlfriend Emilie visited from Arizona for New Year's. The rituals of the thousand-year-old Taos Pueblo were high on our agendas.

It was Christmas Eve, on the heels of winter solstice. Hope and I excitedly made our way past the Pueblo cemetery and into the main plaza, a flat area bordered by ageless five-story adobe and flat-roofed residences; a World Heritage Site. We milled through the growing crowds as the sun went down, tracing the bank of *Ma wha luna,* the small river that originated in the hallowed Blue Lake watershed to the east. The river was life to these peoples who shunned indoor plumbing and electricity. To step foot upon their land was to be humbled.

Anticipation mounted as winter chill took hold. Darkness fell. Neatly stacked towers of pitch wood, from three to twenty feet high, were lit around the plaza. Fires crackled and sparked. Smoke rose as the old bells clanged atop little San Geronimo chapel, signaling the end of vespers and the emergence of the Virgin Mary. Six men carried the Virgin's statue, dressed in white, held high on a dais under a billowing canopy. Rifle-wielding guards stood in front of her, unnoticed until they shot into the air, announcing the Virgin's arrival. Startled onlookers jumped. Small children cried. The celebratory smiles of the unknowing crowd disappeared.

The procession wound deliberately around the eons-old plaza. Fires grew. Drums beat louder. Intermittent rifle reports echoed through dense smoke as the ghostly pageant edged through shadowy darkness. Fire tornadoes leapt from the blazing stacks as the Virgen swayed side to side. Time. Stood. Still.

Some onlookers fell in line behind the procession. Hope and I stood transfixed in the primordial energies that reckoned death and purification, a journey around the Plaza that took us to the edge of Armageddon and brought us back again. I put my arm around Hope. Blessed.

One week later Emilie and I made our way to the Turtle Dance on New Year's Day. It was a ten degrees, a frigid change from her balmy Bisbee home, but she was not deterred. She'd never experienced a Native Pueblo dance. We'd been friends for over thirty years and I was excited to share this day with her. I wondered how the aboriginal event would affect her. She was in the throes of retirement and major life questions. I, on the heels of the Pueblo's Christmas Eve, remained on a soul-stirring high that held undefinable sway.

I picked up the pace from the parking lot as we followed the sound of the drum; drew closer to the bare-chested dancers with white painted chins. Their hot breath steamed and dissipated into the freezing air. The men were adorned in pine boughs; ermine and fox pelts swung from their waists. They wore lacy leggings and bright-feathered headdresses. They shook rattles; their legs, strapped in bells and turtle shells, kept rhythm to the great drum. Solemn women wrapped in bright colored blankets stood in the sunshine and watched.

My eyes moved from the dancers, up and east to their sacred mountain, framed in frosty breath. The hypnotic drum beat forth: one two three, one two three, one two three ... stronger. Louder. One two three raising the vibration, bringing it home and just like that, something deep inside flipped. I knew I was done with s-a-d. Finished.

Emilie and I departed hand in hand. I don't know how, or if, that dance transformed her, but in the wake of my revelation I slept twelve hours that night.

A story is told that Indian women once gathered on the waxing moon to share stories and act as counsel for those who were troubled. The circle offered support and advice with full attention and love. If, however, a woman came to the circle three times with the same problem and no progress, the women of the circle rose and moved, leaving the distressed one alone with her truth.

It was late morning, January 6th. With holiday visitors departed, I headed back to the Pueblo to complete my unforeseen initiation. I normally attended one or two of the dances any given year. I had never attended all three in a row.

Petite Indian women wrapped in multicolored shawls uttered loud, clipped yips from rooftops. A dozen drummers sang and beat hand drums at the end of tightly-grouped dancers – men who wore massive buffalo heads adorned with eagle feathers that twisted and floated as they step-turned with powerful force, as if to taunt the hunters who interspersed them.

It was a spectacle of stirring bodies. The ocher-painted hunters gripped small bows loaded with wooden arrows. Little boys with bows and quivers struggled to keep step among men who danced under deer hides, complete with heads and antlers; pine branches poked from bucks' mouths. The drummers suddenly shifted to a slow trance beat as bison heads and antlers swayed hypnotically. Just as abruptly, the beat quickened. Intensity returned.

The dance ended in front of the kivas, large round rooms dug into the earth. Accessible only by ladder, kivas entailed a climb down, into dark space. Into a metaphorical void. As told by various medicine men and women, it was sacred space, where males once descended to access the powers that women held naturally within their wombs; the place of rites, gestation and mystery.

I did not pretend to know the mythology and history of the Buffalo Dance. It was theirs. I stayed with the symbols that spoke to me in January's womb-dark shadows. In the spirit of the Huntress Artemis, I pondered what ritual I must conjure to ensure my aim was true, as the Huntress and hunted swayed in primordial union. Then I reminded myself that a degree of aimlessness was vital to quest. The place of no answers was the genesis of trust. Freedom began without a plan. This was the unfolding of which Grandmother tree spoke. Let go, let the soul do her work.

I called Montana Ronny the next day. I told her I'd applied for summer forest service jobs. *Perfect* she said. *You, Abbey and Leopold!*

The revelations continued with a spontaneous day trip near Abiquiu. I'd not been there in a decade; my booster shot was overdue. Photographer-friend Robbi steered her BMW up the curvy gravel roads and we came to the dead-end overlook. The White Place: oh my,

I'd forgotten how the piñon-studded hills contrasted the bleached tapestry of rock. Before us spread a hidden canyon lined with spires, the country where Georgia O'Keefe walked the washes and picked up the bones.

We parted company for solo photo shoots. I chose a slot canyon that climbed and narrowed through a series of smooth, water-formed curves. I was unable to negotiate the final tight turns due to ice-laden rock; turned around and headed down. I had long craved loops but learned that to turn around was just as rich; the route back divulged different shadows, angles and views.

I entered an open wash and lay down, all senses awake to sparkling air and dead, rustling cottonwood leaves. A raven's call echoed from white walls. I dug my bare toes into dust and dirt and merged my feral heartbeat with the sky. I stretched my arms outright across the sand. If flesh was my antennae, I wanted to be the biggest danged receiver possible; every atom fused to oneness.

Georgia collected dust in solid form. She carried skulls, femurs and pelvises to her Abiquiu home and painted delicious curves. She captured the bare-bones truth. I rolled onto my belly and grabbed a fistful of dirt. I lifted it to my face and inhaled; stuck out my tongue and tasted time. *Hello, Georgia.*

I liked to think of the White Place as her hideout, where mystery met soul. A secret haunt where the autonomous woman merged with spirit. We all had hideouts. The more the better. Georgia's chattering bones. My talking trees. For those with ears to hear and eyes to see.

Robbi and I made our way down the gravel hill and sped across the highway to Bode's General Store. "Since 1893" it was the Abiquiu lifeline to hardware, feed and groceries. There were skillets the size of a round table top and work gloves packaged by the dozen. I couldn't resist a red-speckled enamelware bowl, perfect for popcorn.

I slept ten hours that night; dreamed my computer was on fire. The insides melted into goo. The image conjured up the caterpillar that liquefied before turning into a butterfly. What dramatic transition was in motion?

While most people checked out the shadow of a remote groundhog on February 2nd, I acknowledged Imbolc, when the winter-faint orb began to feel hot again. The energetic shift was palpable. Shadows shortened, snow thawed and ice broke free. New life quivered below earth's surface, a vibratory tickle impossible to ignore. Feeling antsy, I headed for the rim of the Rio Grande. The trail was soft but not muddy; I found my groove a half mile in.

The trill of the season's first Canyon Wren split the air, a haunting progression of equally-spaced notes that slid down an ethereal scale. I spotted the miniscule bird on a rock outcrop, hopping to high points and calling to convince a little girl wren he was worthy of a pause, a nest site perhaps. He stopped me instead, an untimely distraction on his sex-charged day. How to let him know all was not lost, that his song tingled down my spine and raced my heart, sure as cupid's hit?

A few steps later I came across my first bighorn tracks. I took a seat on a rock and soft focused my eyes, concentrated on general movement rather than small details. There! – across the canyon. A dozen bighorns traversed a steep narrow cleft. I cupped my ears to hear their steps; watched them wind their way out of sight. One ritual remained as the sun faded fast.

I returned to the house and removed the holiday decorations from the solstice tree. A trail of dried needles in my wake, I carried the tree outside, placed it in the fire ring and held a match to its branches. Fire: to mark the end of winter and cast a hallelujah-hello to the sun. I took a seat on an old stump and drummed. The tree transformed to ashes, I sat in the peaceful interlude. Presence. Intention. Soul required little to wed the web of life.

Book events and classes filled to capacity. I connected with old friends and was energized by new ones. I resurrected *Living on the Spine,* my account of five years living solo at the edge of wilderness. Issued twice by publishers, a decade later it was out of print. I obtained the rights, made changes and self-published. The book that had encouraged countless women to break the mold was big as life.

The three months in Taos was the perfect place at the perfect time, yet I could not ignore the familiar urge to hook up Perla and continue down the road. Hitch itch: what's a womad to do? I was within the timeframe I had granted my host for housesitting and I wanted a sign; some indication that my choice to depart was opportune. I returned to the Rio Grande Rim trail.

The morning air was crisp; puffball clouds splattered the Taos sky. Fleeting shadows crossed the sage. A Canyon Wren trilled his heart out. There were fresh bighorn tracks but no sheep. I picked up some scat and pressed it with my fingers – soft and fresh. Teak and I moved toward our favorite overlook to sit a spell.

My eyes scanned rock cliffs as we moved along the trail. Several miles further and almost to the end, I glanced into the gorge, 800-feet down. Nada. I stopped, put down my pack and began to stretch. Bent at the waist, arm in the air, I leaned, turned my head and almost jumped out of my skin. At the end of the promontory, not twenty feet away, were three huge rams with thick curved horns, lazing on a precarious cliffside. I expected them to flee. Bolt toward me the interloper? Down the cliff? At Teak, silent at my side? Instead they stared into my eyes as if to say *Don't let us stop you. Keep stretching.*

Was this real? *Hello* I said, my hand over my racing heart.

I made for my pack and grabbed my camera as Teak looked flummoxed. *Aren't I supposed to bark?* I didn't know how much time I had and I wasn't settling for ass shots. I began to shoot, moving closer and closer, downright ecstatic. I eventually rested the camera against my breasts and sat nearby. Wild animals: my spiritual equivalent of oxygen.

I returned to my stretches, inhaling their presence. They eventually dropped off the point and made a crazy-steep zig-zag down to the Rio. I followed them down a few rolling-rock steps before I reminded myself I was first of all, not a bighorn, and second, I was alone in ankle-twisting territory. I returned to a stable foothold and shot them from above as they trailed down to river's edge to drink. Three graces, in a scene of repose that communicated completion. I had received the sign I asked for. I slept ten hours that night.

Valentine's Day came and went. There was no romantic dinner with a lover. The present teemed with possibility. Lupa howled somewhere in Montana, my muse bayed back and wild encounters did not cease. Teak and I hiked into the Rio Grande Gorge and took a seat by careening water. A dipper perched on a boulder at the head of a cascade. Cold water furled around her as she pumped up and down; an exciting rare close-up of a normally shy bird. Teak's ears perked up and her nose took to the air. I followed her gaze. A bobcat threaded her way down the rocky ridge between sharp volcanic boulders. She came to within ten yards with no obvious concern for us. I had no camera or binocs. It was soul-o me and a feline friend, the first I'd seen since Montana. I reckoned she was back to affirm the headway I'd made. Counting blessings like coup, I made my way up-canyon toward the truck.

Soon thereafter I received word that my cousin Deac was dying of bone cancer. Deac was the son of Aunt Clara, the Danish farmwoman I deemed my second mother. Much older than I, he was a cross between a parent and a brother, and especially close to my Mom. I called him in the hospital. In his salt-of-earth manner he proclaimed he was *gonna ride this horse wherever it takes me.* Now the horse crossed the Iowa prairie and neared the happy hunting grounds.

Distance is a strange companion to mourning. I snowshoed up to Grandmother Tree. Heavy-hearted, I asked her to deliver my love; to cloak him in peace. When all is vibration, everything is possible. I sat beneath her boughs and reviewed memories of Deac, like the sunny day we drove across the Iowa heartland, searching for gravestones in small rural cemeteries that might reveal his father's identity.

Even in death, all is alive, Grandmother Tree imparted. *Are you ready to step outside the door?* I awoke the next morning at 4:00 with an auditory dream: a door creaked opened. Deac died that day. I stepped into the frosty air, made a fire and drummed. With Deac's affable spirit set free, I recalled the still dark morning he let ten-year-old me order pie for breakfast at the local Maid-Rite.

Taos-time waned as I followed the call to curve southwest and expand book tour into Arizona. I walked the Chamisa plateaus celebrated in John Nichols' prose. I was trying to get a bead on *the door,* and the aromatic sagebrush hills were the perfect place.

I rubbed pungent sage leaves between my fingers and held them to my nose. I recalled the day, years back, when I'd observed an amoeba-like cloud. Bats? Insects? I pulled over and parked; struggled up a loose-dirt embankment to watch. Blurred movement sharpened into flutter as the cloud arrived. There I stood, smack in the middle of a gasp-gorgeous monarch migration, on their way to Michoacán. Cars sped by. Incredible to think I was the only one to stop. To bless the silky wings. I smiled. A *milagro* John would say. A miracle.

One never knew when one might happen upon a phenomenon of wings or hooves, fins or shells. I had witnessed the miles-long journey of millions of wildebeest, zebra and gazelle on the African savannah. I'd seen Trumpeter Swans, Sandhill Cranes, Snow Geese, Mexican free-tailed bats and lady bugs answer the seasonal call to move. I'd shared the salt-water marvels of migrating salmon, whales and turtles; watched as hundreds of elk coated the frosty plains.

The planet is woven in migration flaps, thuds, swishes, splashes and sonar sounds beyond our reach, and yes, the silence of nocturnal passage. To step into such force, knowingly or not, is initiation. Entry into transformative vibration. Participation in one's own salvation.

Our work is to move beyond the door and define our personal medicine – our unique contribution to the planet; the gift we unfurl on our personal migration across this lifetime.

When I first moved to Taos in 1999, I wrote that the tension of a community that perched between 13,000-foot peaks and an 800-foot gorge would be palpable. It was true. Ancient grievances and vendettas between Natives and Spanish permeated the environment, energies that many newcomers would never grasp. Anglos were primarily a 1900s addition as socialite Mabel Dodge Luhan, author DH Lawrence and a flood of eastern artists made Taos their home. Today's Taos is an artistic, engaging, spiritual, rustic, primarily Catholic, downright complicated community where rundown trailers sit next to multi-million-dollar adobe homes. Taos boasts a healthy dark side and a temperament to match the Day-Glo sunsets. A writer's dream. An artist's trance. She is her own homeopathic remedy; her soft adobe homes heal like a mud poultice on her ancient wounds.

I departed April 1st, daring the goddess of jokes. I loved this day of pranks born from the old Roman festival of Hilaria. I'd played my share on Hope and friends.

All Perla systems were a go until I pressed the button on the fridge. It was dead as a doornail. I checked the propane and the electricity. I backed off and gave it time to change its mind. Nada. No joke. I hooked up Perla and turned her around in a nearby field. Perhaps the movement would jiggle air pockets. Still nada. A phone call to the manufacturer and green dust by the coils told the tale of an ammonia leak. The fridge was a goner and would need to be replaced to the tune of $1400. Not funny. I considered a regular one, but RV fridges were designed for the nomad life, to weather bumps and run on electricity or propane. Imperative for my backcountry boondock life. I filled the cooler with ice and prepared to head down the road. Surely something would come to light. It always did.

We rolled south, once more in travel mode. I'd slowly rounded the renowned Taos horseshoe and began the winding descent toward Pilar when my eyes started to water. My nose burned. Teak began to whine. The truck gauges read normal but something was seriously wrong. Desperate, I opened the windows and stuck out my head as I struggled to keep Blue and Perla on the road. It seemed like an hour to get down that ten-minute stretch. I pulled over at the bottom and Teak and I bailed. I was dizzy and nauseous and gasped for breath. The cab was filled with fumes but I couldn't find the source.

Windows down, I began to drive again. I stopped a few miles down the road and looked harder. It took four stops, digging deeper and deeper, to unearth a canister of bear spray that had leaked into gas and goo in the bottom of a plastic box. Holy jezus. My phone rang.

It was Joe, who had given me the canister on a hike to Jewel Basin in Montana. How the hell did events line up like this?

Joe knew the drill. A canister had once gone off in his apartment. In a calm I've-got-your-back voice, he told me to wipe everything down, including the steering wheel. *Wipe with what?* My brain was fuzzy. Joe reminded me I was hitched to a fully-equipped trailer. He said to expect a headache; eye burn would last for a couple of days. Twitching and traumatized, I ditched the plastic box in a gas station garbage bin. I didn't care what else was in it. I wanted it gone.

Lungs afire, I continued down the road. I made my way through Albuquerque and south on I-25, stopping occasionally for air and to wipe away more film. I kept talking to Teak to make sure she was okay. I exited on the San Antonio turnoff for Bosque del Apache. There was an RV park by the boundary but I saw a gravel road that looked promising for a boondock. I took a sharp right and found a beautiful desert spot; kept visualizing clean lungs and sharp thinking. That's when I started to spit blood.

My headache barely registered the next morning. I tested my lungs with a short bike ride. I had no problems catching my breath but the sting persisted. I unfolded the camp chair, sat in the desert morn with my journal. I had escaped a big one. Hilaria, eh?

I phoned Kevin, the manager at Bosque del Apache whom I had interviewed by phone earlier in the year. He offered me a tour behind the gated roads, something I'd craved for decades. The stars of the Bosque – 100,000 wintering Snow Geese and Sandhill Cranes – had winged their way north weeks earlier but it mattered not. The day garnered three bobcats, large herds of mule deer and fifty-plus wild turkeys. We stood on the edge of the Rio Grande as he pointed out new measures for flow control and a salt cedar eradication project. A lone coyote skulked across a field, trailing a very plump skunk.

A few Snow Geese appeared at dusk; dabblers broke the mirrored waters. I leaned against the truck for stability and clicked the shutter. Without the grand display of mass ascension the brain and body settled down; sought messages of a different kind, like seasonal movement, migration and those left behind. I made one more round of the preserve as night fell. A mountain lion and her cub crossed the road and disappeared into the forest. A young Kestrel cried for her mother.

Susan and I had been best friends for over a decade. We met in Taos when she took my women's handgun class. As far as I knew, she was the only friend who slept like me, with a gun and a vibrator next to her bed. Our sisterhood had teemed with biking, hiking, shooting and Super Bowl parties, with an occasional revenge shopping spree thrown in for good measure. Sue had recently purchased a travel van and we were set to meet at Elephant Butte for three days.

It blew like a typhoon up there on the butte. When weather socked me in I usually snuggled up, lit candles and wrote. Not so with Susan parked a few feet away. What a shame – we were trapped inside to reminisce, swill wine and laugh til our sides hurt. Womads. We were a different ilk, and although I was the only one who had taken to the road full-time, we were similar in chutzpah and not much matched our irreverence.

Our time together in the rearview mirror, we hugged farewell. There was no telling when I would see her again. I knew only too well that every hello contained an inherent goodbye, but it didn't salve the sadness. She headed north to Santa Fe and I pointed south. I hoped to find a New Mexico boondock but nothing tempted me. Before I knew it I was in Arizona coming up on the turnoff for one of my favorite stops: Hot Well Dunes. It was Sunday night. The ATV crowds were gone.

It'd been eight years since my last visit. It was low-key lovely as ever. There were two hot pools framed by dunes and rock and a small streamside cottonwood bosque. A few campers were secreted around corners. It seemed everyone wanted the same peace and quiet that I sought. I parked on the far side of some mesquite trees, got out and heaved a sigh of relief. A cardinal hopped among the thorny bushes, trilling for all he was worth. Yes Sir Scarlet, it was worth the extra exhausting miles.

The nearest camper was a little Scamp. I'd just freed Teak and Hobo when a sweet cowboy – hat, vest, boots and an impressive waxed handlebar mustache – popped out of that little trailer. *Hello, ma'am* he said with a smile and a drawl. We talked later in the bathing-suits-required pools. Turned out Lon was from Tres Piedras, a little town not far from Taos. He invited me to share some grilled steak but I politely declined. I wasn't up for a chit-chat or other complications.

I placed my quartz crystal in the spring to charge overnight before I returned to the pools and the full moonrise. I had the water to myself as I pulled my bathing suit down to my waist and soaked in silence. Another chain of self-promotion and friends would coalesce in Bisbee. Quiet interludes were a necessity.

I returned to Perla through enchanting moon shadows. Somewhere out there lurked Hobo. I wondered how he would manage the night with the coyotes, bobcats and javelina. There was no keeping him inside on warm nights, any more than I could keep the womadic tides from encircling my soul.

Hobo magnificat bounded through the door at dawn. I collected my crystal from the stream and dipped into the hot well for one last soak. Lon ducked through the doorway of his little trailer and handed me a card. *Here's my phone number* he said. *Give a call if you have any trouble on the road.* The gentleman meant every word. I packed up Perla and gave that crystal a few pings with the tuner. It vibrated me off the bed as I set my sites on Whitewater Draw, an out-of-the-way wildlife refuge.

I cherished Whitewater Draw for its nondescript beauty and simple infrastructure. It was the kind of place where you never heard a weed eater. I had visited for years; written articles about her special magic. I knew where the three varieties of owls nested and had watched as twenty thousand wintering Sandhill Cranes filled the shallow pools at dusk. I'd witnessed hundreds of Yellow-headed Blackbirds swell the rushes at dawn; frozen my fingers and butt in anticipation of the winter solstice sun. My heart warmed with the memory of two years earlier, when I taught a nature writing workshop in the old pole barn. A Great Horned Owl had roosted directly above on the rafters, stared down with glowing golden eyes.

I had the Draw to myself. I pulled into the small circular camping area and headed for the dirt trail. Like Bosque del Apache, the cranes had migrated, abandoning the oasis to the long-billed ones. White-faced Ibis, Avocets and Godwits waded the shallows; fed gracefully from murk and mud.

Back in Perla for siesta, I glanced at my phone and the one scant bar of connection. An email had slipped in from Colorado Humanities asking if I was going to attend the banquet for the Colorado Book Award Finalists. *What?* I was on the phone in a nanosecond.

Are you saying I'm a finalist?

Why, yes. The written letters were sent out days ago. It was a tough decision. You're in great company.

Written letter? Snail mail hadn't caught up. Holy cow! My life had just changed at sweet little Whitewater Draw. I stepped outside and let out a whoop as I skip-hopped up the road ... something to do with cloud nine. I was finally recognized for all of those nose-to-the-grindstone years. The mountains of rejection letters. *Drive Me Wild!* I flashed back to those two badgers. Ya, baby.

I returned to find a forty-foot 5th wheel parked a few feet from Perla. Kids' plastic toys were strewn around its periphery. I shook it off and went inside to share the book news with friends; had just picked up the phone when I was enveloped by the sound of a dull bass drum. *Gawd give me strength.* The vibration turned out to be kids running up and down the inside of the 5th wheel. I went over and knocked.

A sweet woman stepped outside. I didn't start with the noise. I began with Whitewater Draw. Had they been there before? Could I help them? I was a full-timer. Then her story. Full-timing had been their dream and they had finally found the courage to sell their house, buy the 5th wheel and take to the road. They had recently departed their Kansas home. They were homeschooling six children: mixed race adopted kids. She had no idea of the vibration from the kids running. The noise ended with that knowledge as my fascination began.

The kids filed outside like ducklings the next morning, inquisitive and mannerly as could be. I offered to take them on a nature walk. Their eyes lit up. We rounded the ponds as I pointed out the wading birds, Scarlet Tanagers and Yellow Warblers in the trees. The mating pair of Great Horned Owls in the barn. I offered the older ones photography tips. I was their biology class and they bubbled with questions. Truth was, I learned more from them that day. When I see RVs and homeschoolers, I offer myself as writer, photographer or naturalist. Their choice.

Book award finalist. Creative nonfiction. I continued my spring romp toward Bisbee. My forever-friend Emilie and her husband Paul were in the process of breaking up. I couldn't help but wonder if that Pueblo dance had worked some magic for Em as well as me! Still and all, it was hard. I loved them both and while I understood the necessity it still sucked. There I was ready to celebrate; there they were in turmoil.

The Bisbee library was standing room only for the wild encounters talk and slideshow. My freedom life on the road resonated as did the planet's potential to heal our weary souls. I shared that twenty minutes a day of bare feet on the earth delivered a stress-reducing electron wash which reduced the free radicals inside our body; the nasty critters that damaged cells and contributed to cancer. Science was catching up with the mystics.

Postscript. Tired of making ice at Emilie's, I broke down and bought a new refrigerator.

I headed to Sedona to meet bear-spray Joe, who had recently claimed his identity and walked the world a proud gay man. Sedona had no boondock spots; the landscape was one of the most tightly managed I had experienced, right down to paid parking areas for trailheads. We each paid $60 a night, a record amount, to camp in a serene RV park at the edge of town.

Sedona. Red rock country. A renowned healing vortex, it attracts healers and spiritual seekers from around the world, authentic and charlatans alike. The streets are lined with crystal shops and chakra readers. Joe and I hiked miles up a secluded canyon on a sweat-hot day, only to meet pink Jeeps full of tourists. Another hike into the red stone country began with a flute player perched on a high rock chimney. I couldn't help but think he was employed by the Chamber of Commerce.

We switched to a more spacious and secluded RV spot in the park the second day. Hobo wasn't around for the move but the place wasn't that big and I figured he'd find me. He didn't. He was gone. I walked the park calling him. The people who took my old spot said he'd meowed at their door several times, despite their three large aggressive dogs. He didn't show up that night. I made the rounds the next morning. I was headed back to Perla when a man walked toward me carrying the marmalade orange one. He said Hobo had approached him as he walked down the road, lay down in front of him and rolled over. *Stop! Pick me up! Help!* It worked.

Dang Hobo! You scared me to death. Hobo planted himself in Perla's doorway and didn't venture out beyond the picnic table. Teak, on the other hand, remained her perfect self: quiet, obedient and sweet as could be. *Best dog in the world.*

Joe towed south and I turned north toward a much-loved boondock. Southern Utah, near Bluff, offered red rock spiral beauty, solace and seclusion. I opened the door on a bold purple sunset as silence pressed against my breast. A lone mariposa lily reached from the sand. Yes indeed, I was back. Teak slept under the stars as I took to the bed for a long, silent slumber. Hobo prowled.

I awoke at dawn. First light defined fissures, shadows and ravines. Contrast waned as the sun rose higher, until midday brightness flattened stone monoliths into one dimensional sheets of rock; erased character, and left only a hint of the centuries of wind that carved a crevasse. The noonday landscape is like a monotonous life. That's why we need movement. To keep the shadows alive.

Hobo hunted lizards as Teak and I walked a boulder-strewn wash and turned up a scree mountainside to a sandy plateau. I took off my top as I sang my way down cliffside to soak in oasis pools. Teak waded as I lay on the rock and closed my eyes. A wave of exhaustion caught me off guard. Did I catch a glimpse of tiredness in the peripatetic life, the constant push down the road? I knew I could not keep to the road forever, but at what point would I shift gears? I sometimes imagined myself in a little casita, a part-time base from which to travel. I didn't have a clue how that would materialize, or if I really wanted it to.

I returned to Perla and lay down on the bed. The phone suddenly rang but there were no bars. *It's Bonnie Day with the Prescott National Forest. Are you still interested in a summer temp position?*

It was May. They wanted me in June. I said yes with one caveat: a week off for the Colorado Book Awards. I put down the phone as my affirmative answer took an opposite swing. A fulltime job, what about my writing? Backtrack south to Arizona? Turning around was not my MO. Hell, I wondered if I was employable at this point in my life.

I noted the obvious pluses: a wildscape to explore, new know-how and steady income. I called friends who reminded me it was a seasonal position, not a life sentence. Ronny's *You, Leopold and Abbey* reverberated in my ears. They'd taken a similar bend in the road. Lest I forget: *spirit puts me where I need to be.*

With three weeks until start day, I high-tailed it over Wolf Creek Pass and into the San Luis Valley for book tour. I reunited with friends in Crestone against a backdrop of more personal upheaval. Lynn had accused me of bad behavior while parked at her house.

Sometimes truth telling was bad behavior. I'll own that. Having just departed Montana Bud, I had zero tolerance for watching a sister sing a destructive tune with her man. I knew him. We had gotten along fine in the past but I'd kept a distance. Now I witnessed him dealing drugs on her property when she was absent, and he was playing loud music next door to Perla, ten feet from my head at midnight. He ignored my polite requests to turn it down. I tolerated the music several nights before I appeared in Lynn's kitchen and asked for music boundaries – to set times that worked for him and me. She said I had no right. Her house, her rules. I was stunned. When I mentioned the drugs to Lynn she said *He isn't using cuz he'd told me so.* The ex-con was conning her.

Months after my departure she did tell him to leave. Her anger at me, however, remained intact. Sometimes the messenger is flat out ignored, sometimes the messenger is heeded, sometimes the messenger gets a stake in the heart.

Wolf Creek Pass was in flames. I was one of the last vehicles to make it over before the highway closed; was still a little shaky when I arrived at Kiz's cabin. We'd been friends since the early 1990's, during my years at Dancing Raven, several miles up the road. Many an afternoon we puffed an American Spirit in her Crestone garden; blew smoke as we shared stories, dreams and guffaws.

Kiz's coffee perked away in an old aluminum pot. We hugged, she sat me down, handed me a cup and looked me in the eye.

There's something I need to tell you, Christina.

Oh fuck, not a second sister-ambush.

Years ago you came into my life with all your wildness and wisdom just when I needed to break free and be myself. I want to thank you. I want to be sure you know how life-changing that was for me. How important your wildness was and still is.

I sat before the formidable woman with long black hair and cried. I respected Kiz as much as anyone. She had just brought me to my metaphorical knees.

Kizzen laughed: *You're the kind of woman that when you come up the driveway the man of the house runs to lock the door.*

Another good epitaph.

I completed a Crestone book event and moved a few miles north to Valley View Hot Springs, a clothing-optional favorite. I'd soaked in the mountainside pools for three decades, lingering with deer and bats and the occasional snake that slithered by my feet in the water. Rare fireflies blinked brilliant yellow at streamside as the vast high desert unrolled below my eight-thousand-foot perch. Nope. There was no place like the San Luis Valley. Its hoar frost winters took no prisoners. Its immensity opened the chest and laid the spirit bare, revealing up to four weather cells at one time, from sunshine to hail to lightning-riddled clouds. I'd experienced it all from the steamy water and my home a few miles away, Dancing Raven.

I climbed on my bike and pedaled the gravel road along the Sangre de Cristo foothills. It was time to return to my cabin. I crossed Major Creek drainage and skirted familiar patches of aspen. The road still boasted agonizing stutter bumps on the curvy, uphill climbs. I pulled up to the closed gate. I had placed the cabin well: a view of the valley yet privacy from the road. My turquoise hand-painted gate rotted on the ground, the splintered wood replaced with metal. The mailbox I had planted twenty years earlier, however, still stood. I parked the bike in the ditch and began the mile trek as memories flooded the brain. This was the place where two new lovers – silence and solitude – had introduced themselves and rocked my life.

Red paintbrush dotted the high desert slope. I recognized the lone sagebrush where I once picked and bundled smudge sticks. I rounded the corner and stopped. There they were, my seven-sided log cabin and her guardian tree, the old piñon. Welcome home, Christina.

I stepped onto the deck and knocked on the wooden double doors. A middle-aged woman turned from her desk, stood and moved toward me with a growing smile. *Christina* she said. *I always knew you would show up.* I'd not met her before yet she knew who I was. *Living on the Spine* was on her window sill.

Lisa welcomed me inside as I walked in my footsteps of long ago. Despite one owner in between us, the cabin's simplicity and beauty was as I had left it. I stared up at the beams, touched the center tree trunk that supported it all. I'd forgotten the earthy eloquence. I was amazed at the marvel I had created.

We walked the rolling land as I pointed out the location for the well I had permitted with the county. I showed her where my medicine wheel had been. Christina Spring still flowed. The mountain lilac was in bloom and my Grandma Nealson's peony bush had a gigantic bud. I enjoyed this woman who, like myself, was from the Midwest. The land could not have chosen a better keeper.

I have often asked myself how I left everything behind to build this place at the edge of wilderness. What did I *do* for five years? The imperative was to live free of roles, to discover true self. Women so rarely get the opportunity to find out who we are outside of professions, relationships and others' expectations. Given a window, we are often too guilty and fearful to take the time for ourselves.

I had intended to live alone for one year, through the four seasons. Instead I stayed for five. I sat, listened and observed. I journaled every day, slept with darkness and rose with the dawn to see my frosty breath. The beginning of every month I drew a large circle on newsprint and wrote the days of the month clockwise. On that mandala I charted the full and new moons, dreams, moods, pre-menstrual days, bleeding days and ovulation. I learned how dreams and moods corresponded with monthly and seasonal cycles. I noted migrations: the first Nighthawk of spring, the last bat to fly south.

It was as if my soul knew the opportunity would not come again. I was ferocious with *NO,* enforced strong boundaries and lost friends because of it, even if they were close by. Every night I sat in the medicine wheel, four white stones that designated the four directions, and watched the sun sink behind the Cochetopa Hills to the west. Every morning I watched sun's light defeat shadow and slip nearer to the cabin. I learned to see reality as metaphor. And in true Celtic spirit, I made friends with the numen – the sacred spirits of the land. Springs, ponds, rock, groves and a male ghost that frequented a certain part of the land below the hitching post. My days at Dancing Raven were the genesis of my understanding that everything was vibration, and through that vibration, we were one.

How did I leave my married, professional life behind and disappear into a solitary landscape for five years? My most obvious answer is that Chris left Boulder for Guatemala one day. She met a jaguar in the jungle and returned as Christina. She moved to the San Luis Valley. Once there, she purchased a piece of earth zoned "wasteland."

I departed Dancing Raven with Lisa's invitation to visit any time. I walked down the lane and glanced over to the ravine on the left, where the claret cup cacti bloomed every spring, a small patch of scarlet across the high desert foothill. The thrill of that discovery returned every time I saw one.

One week remained before I reported to work in Prescott. I continued up the San Luis Valley, dropped over Poncha Pass and into Salida. I finished book tour with a full-house reading before I turned southwest. Then, in a fit of bravery or insanity, I chose a glorious, adrenaline-charged romp through the Colorado high country. I connected the dots between Ouray, Silverton and Durango as I ticked off tight, steep and devastatingly beautiful mountain passes: Monarch. Red Mountain. Molas. Coal Bank. Mancos. One hell of a heavenly day.

Mancos Pass was the smallest and signaled five short miles from my night's destination. I chugged up the highway at sunset, rounded the corner and POP! – pound pound pound – a flat tire. It was my first while towing, at the top of the pass, on a deadly curve where three lanes converged into two. I sat tight and fought panic as I considered my options. The day's deadly highways flashed before me. *If this had happened earlier …*

I was on the phone to my emergency service when knuckles rapped against my closed window. A thirty-ish man with a crew cut asked if *they* could help. Another man and two little boys stood on the opposite side of the truck.

I'm okay. I've got this.

We can change it for you he said.

No telling how long I'd wait on the top of the darkening perilous curve. It was time to trust.

The guys instructed their young sons to stand in the safety of the ditch and proceeded to park their pickups behind my trailer with blinkers on. They collected the jack and tire iron from their tools when we couldn't figure out if the trailer had one. *Some do, some don't* they said. These guys were good! When they squatted by the tire and strained to loosen the lugs I saw pistols holstered on their waists next to badges. It turned out they were off-duty officers parked on the pass when they heard the blowout. One had jurisdiction on the Cortez side and the other on the Hesperus side; one was going to work, one was just off his shift.

Nice Glock I said. He said he always carried it.

Me too I said.

You travel with a gun? That's good!

My armed angels had me rolling down the pass in minutes.

An impromptu meeting with Mancos friends and a parking spot by their house was followed the next night in a peace-full forest outside of Flagstaff. As serendipity would have it, a USFS woman escorted me to her favorite secluded boondocking spot. I told her I was on my way to Prescott to be like her. She laughed and wished me luck.

Teak, Hobo and I walked the isolated forest road as I soaked up my final night of unstructured time. If I had won the Megamillions drawing that night I would not change a thing. Me, the womad minimalist.

I arrived at the Prescott Chamber of Commerce on a Sunday afternoon. I was exhausted, knew no one and had one day to get settled. Not the best planning. I grabbed a city map and a local guide to RV parks and began to search for a place to plop. With work demands I would need hook-ups, laundry facilities and a safe place for Teak and Hobo. Spiritual demands were different: beauty, proximity to hiking and quiet.

I called a couple of prospects on the edge of town. The first one was a sardine-nightmare. The second was situated among scenic Tom Mix rocks called the Dells and walking distance to a lake. It was low key, had little infrastructure (read: few kids) and had one spot available for long term. I grabbed it. Hobo was one of several cats in the 'hood and Teak had scenic trails to walk and sniff. The family was happy.

I reported to the Forest Service office the next morning, a drab array of rooms that housed the administrative core, including my supervisor. Forest techs were in the basement with no windows. Imagine my thrill to discover I would work out of a log cabin at the edge of Prescott's urban Granite Mountain Wilderness, ten minutes from the RV park. With one week's orientation under my belt, I left Teak and Hobo with Perla, in the care of neighbors, and headed to Aspen for the Colorado Book Award presentation.

It'd been two decades since my last visit to Aspen, a wild women's backpack trip to Conundrum Hot Springs that culminated in a naked hike above treeline. I checked into my motel and took to historic streets; downed a latte in the homey bookstore that had once hosted a packed-house reading for *Living on the Spine.* The unforgettable night I met my tennis heroine, Martina Navratilova; when a lover from the past had stood in line to get his book signed and surprised me. It felt fantastic to be back.

Decked out, excited and nervous, I entered the hall and began to mingle. I'd never been much of a schmoozer and this was no exception. A few introductions were all I could manage before I sat with three friends to await the award presentation. Alas, my name was not called. The creative nonfiction award went to Harrison Fletcher: *Descanso for My Father*. I congratulated Harrison and thanked the Colorado Humanities folks who had sponsored the award. This recognition had changed my life. I beamed, told them I'd be back another year, and headed out with friends.

We celebrated my nomination with champagne at the base of the Maroon Bells. The Bells were as treacherous as they were spectacular; fourteen-thousand footers I'd not attempted to climb and knew, at this point in life, I never would. I'd once scrambled and struggled up many of Colorado's fifty-eight fourteeners; peaked out on a dozen before lightening-laced monsoons forced a descent. Mountains humbled me. They taught me how to lean; stood me upright-naked on top of the world.

I stared at the Bells as my friends took off on a lake trail. I wish I'd won. Of course I did. Then down those mountains rolled a revelation: I *had* won, weeks earlier, the night I read with finalists at the Denver Press Club. That trip from Tucson to Denver had launched an unforeseen reunion with three of my once-closest woman friends, Jacqueline, Carole and Lori.

It had been thirty years since we shared stories, ritual and dance. Within our Boulder sisterhood we had hatched dreams via drumbeat, far afield of the traditional old boys' club. Through our years together we learned to trust our higher calling. Natives called it the medicine path. Others called it karmic slate. I called it soul intention: what the soul completes through us in this lifetime. The secret, and here was the hard part, was to stay out of the soul's way.

The group came to a natural end after several years. Carole, a midwife, became a well-known homeopath. Jacqueline, also a midwife, switched careers and traveled the globe on behalf of world peace. Lori fulfilled her dream to become a filmmaker. She interviewed indigenous women around the globe and created *Arise!*, an award winning film that portrayed heroic struggles in the face of climate change. I, a women's psychotherapist, moved to the San Luis Valley to live in wilderness solitude and commence my writing life.

We three surrendered to muse. Muse, from muein, "to initiate someone into mysteries."

There they were for my reading in a memorable twist of fate. I'd spent a night with each, ending with Lori in her brownstone, every room a reflection of her spirit, decorated with art and symbols from around the world. It was as if we'd never lost touch as we shared our lives, right down to relationship struggles and alcoholic men. We spoke of the passion for our next projects; she gave me a copy of *Arise!*, I gave her *Drive Me Wild*. Lori drove me to DIA the next morning, a rush hour trip that passed way too fast. Where are traffic jams when you want one? We kissed goodbye and promised to stay in close touch.

My prize: sisterhood reunion.

Lori died of lung cancer within three years; a ferociously fast takedown of an indubitable goddess. A woman whose quest was not to be denied: with the help of her daughter she unplugged the hospital tubes and hired an ambulance to transport her into the mountains to die, surrounded by loved ones and her cat.

My USFS orientation continued as I obtained my official driver's license and truck. Off work at 4:00, I returned to Teak and Hobo and the special place where we were parked. Outside the door were granite mounds and stunning formations. We walked daily through narrow ponderosa and oak dotted ravines. It was the land of the granite spirits. The earth brimmed with pit house remnants of early cultures - axe heads, points, pottery. There was an immovable staccato to these lands.

Phainopeplas (the black cardinal of the desert) zipped from piñon treetops. A gregarious family of ravens competed with Hobo for ownership of the two-legged hearts. Waterfalls of teensy new-hatched quail flowed over rock as tarantulas made their hairy-legged way across coarse dirt. Soft cottontails, the primo arbitrators of thorns, gentled the sandpaper rock.

My temporary home was the perfect balance to early work starts and finishes. My neighbors were fun and thoughtful. Brandon the frisbee player, Gail the nurse, Bill the Buddha intellect. Every morning I jumped into the green 4WD pickup and headed miles into the dispersed camping hinterlands to be the Forest Service eyes, watching for illegal ATV roads. I answered campers' questions, handed out literature, picked up garbage and yes, Walmart bags of shit. I traveled the back roads to the Verde River and high into the Juniper Mountains of the Prescott National Forest. I was soon to discover, however, that this re-location was not about my rec tech position. It was about fire, the death of nineteen hotshots, and a tree that would not let me go.

Thor himself took center stage, hurling lightning bolts at Prescott's wind-whipped mountains. I had barely returned from Aspen, growing accustomed to the badge, belted pants and what-do-you-call-that-shade-of-green truck. I was reassigned for a day in town to learn the developed recreation sites. A co-worker and I hurried to finish the fee collections as huge raindrops splotched the windshield. The truck dispatch radio erupted with chatter as seven lightning-sparked fires flared in the drought-parched mountains around town.

The winding asphalt road turned shiny with sheets of rain as we sought a higher vantage point to watch. Storms in the Southwest were patchy. One could drive in and out of several within a matter of minutes. We called in a new plume of smoke as I glanced out the passenger window to see a bellowing cloud explode above the bone-dry mountains to the south. *Oh my Gawd, the Yarnell fire just blew up!*

The village of Yarnell was an hour's drive south. The small blaze had hardly made the news. A lightning-caused fire on state land, it was supposed to have been out the day before. I grew edgy; kept glancing south over my shoulder as the pink and white pyrocumulonimbus cloud heaved up with a sinister surge. Unbeknownst to us, Flagstaff meteorologists had contacted Yarnell fire personnel with early warnings that our Prescott storm had Yarnell in its sights, with severe wind shifts and 60 mph gusts.

The *New York Times* headline popped into my inbox around 7:00 p.m. "Fast-Moving Blaze Kills 19 Firefighters in Central Arizona." My heart stopped as I clicked on the link and scanned: wildland firefighters … Yarnell.

Prescott's Granite Mountain Hotshots were dead. I rose from my chair, shoved open the door and raced to the top of a nearby hill, staring west to their namesake Granite Mountain. Three weeks into my new position, Prescott and I were hurled into shock. It was a small community. Everyone knew these men and their families, if not personally, then as members of their churches, from hanging out in a local bar, watching them bicycle up the street. My co-workers and the Forest Service hotshots, whose trucks and offices were a few yards from my office, went numb. Tears were openly shed as Prescott grieved for "their boys." The Forest Service sent counselors for employees, as tributes flooded in from around the world. My second supervisor, Pete, had trained with the crew and fought fires with them. The pain turned me inside out. I was a part of the tragedy by default, a severe test to my belief that spirit puts me where I need to be.

Granite Mountain, the centerpiece of a twenty-nine-year-old wilderness in the Prescott National Forest, was a far cry from the vast and verdant Rocky Mountains I was accustomed to. There were no snowcapped peaks; no soft green tundra and wind-whipped krummholz at tree line. Rugged Granite Mountain rose stark and sharp, her face resembling that of an acne-pockmarked kid.

Granite, a mix of quartz and feldspar, had long been worshipped for its sacred powers connected to the sea and to its multi-colored striated earth. Egyptians believed it balanced mind, body and spirit. They included it in their pyramids. Climbers say this particular mountain's rock quality rivaled Yosemite's. What I can tell you is this mountain cast a strong spell. The Granite Mountain Hotshots had obviously felt the same.

Hotshot crews maintained an ultimate brotherhood bond. They were a firefighting machine of 20 people: 40 arms 40 legs 20 heads and one brain, the superintendent's. He called the shots and the crew placed all trust in him. He was assisted in the field by the assistant superintendent, squad bosses (three) and senior crew men (two). They stood ready to take one another's places should the need arrive.

Details of the firestorm unfolded with horror. As the fire had rushed toward Yarnell, the smoke plume grew to a colossal 40,000 feet. The Granite Mountain Hotshots were the only remaining crew on the fireline. At 4:04 they were safely in the black, a burned-over safe zone on a high ridge. Everyone assumed they had retreated off the mountain to safety. They hadn't. In a horrific turn of events, they abandoned safety and fought their way downhill through tangled manzanita into a box canyon.

To come upon a manzanita bush in the desert is to meet a living sculpture. Its slick and shiny mahogany branches twist into stunning lines, in lovely contrast to its evergreen leaves. There is no symmetry to this plant that dominates the chaparral landscape. Its branches interlock in patterns of wild unkempt beauty. And it's incendiary. It creates a heavy, tough impenetrable thicket that explodes into killer torches when dry and ignited. Its nickname is gasoline on a stick.

The official report left haunting images. The Granite Mountain Hotshots' radio cries for help hit the airwaves as seventy-foot flames raced toward them, covering one hundred yards in nineteen seconds. A tanker loaded with flame retardant desperately searched, but no one knew where they'd gone.

Given the Hotshots' chain of command, I believed that someone ordered those men out of the safety of the black, but no one was talking, including the lookout, the only survivor, who had fled his position on a nearby hill in the wake of oncoming flames. With no satisfactory answers forthcoming from the human world, I decided to search for the ancient tree the Hotshots had saved a few days earlier. Perhaps truth could be found under her seventy-foot canopy, in quiet reverence to the unspeakable events on Yarnell Hill.

While I was in Aspen the manmade Doce Fire fire ripped over mountain ridges, destroying 6,767 acres of the Granite Mountain Wilderness. The cowardly shooter using incendiary targets was never identified.

My supervisor had contacted the Hotshots to alert them to a very special tree on Granite Mountain. Considered a cultural treasure, she was likely 2000 years old. Her trunk was eighteen feet in diameter. At fifty feet tall, she was the largest alligator juniper in the country. The Hotshots answered the call to save her. She was my destination.

It took a keen eye for off-trail tracking and three tries to find her. She stood apart, off-trail, along a wash lined with fire-charred trees. Her far-reaching silhouette was sobering. Teak and I approached the tree and sat at her majestic base.

The Hotshots' work was obvious. Sawed bushes and tree stumps lay on the ground. Flame had traveled to their fire line and stopped as her nearby progeny burned into blackened skeletons. While some Hotshots removed ladder fuels at her base, others climbed with water bottles to dowse a burning limb. Haunting photos remain of that day, when they formed a pyramid in front of her massive trunk and snapped jubilant memories of their accomplishment.

I removed my boots and leaned against her trunk; pushed my bare toes into the ground and entered her world. Juniper's days were enveloped in towhee, jay and woodpecker calls; the presence of visitors like me who journeyed to pay homage. Her creek-fed power had swelled for centuries under the Milky Way, as bear, lion and bobcat threaded past her holy presence. Sentinel and storyteller to her Mother, Granite Mountain, this tree had witnessed eons.

A pesky bee broke the reverie. It buzzed around my head and finally landed on my feet. I smiled at the tiny messenger as a Red-tailed Hawk cry stroked the sky. The Ancient One spoke:

Write your truth, Christina. You are safe and sound.

Questers know: The search for truth is perilous. The expression of truth more so. Her counsel penetrated my soul. *Safe and sound* felt like a premonition, a piece of advice to be tucked away.

I closed my eyes and envisioned the boys' dirt-smudged faces. I heard their laughter as the yellow-shirted saviors dropped to their hands and knees and climbed onto one another's backs in a fit of celebration. As if to join, I stepped into the wide opening between the tree's massive multiple trunks. Then, silence. They were gone. I stepped from the tree.

According to Doug Hulmes, professor of environmental studies at Prescott College, the Swedish word for a sacred or significant tree, naturminne upptecknare, translates as "recorder of nature's memory." Mother Mountain and her ancient juniper, in ageless service to muse Mneme, bestowed the Hotshots' spirits to memory. They asked only that we step up. Move closer to the alligator patterned bark and listen. She was resolute in her uproar: *There is no grace without truth.*

I wrote a thirty page article and put it in a drawer. I had my hunches of how things had unfolded on Yarnell Hill, but it would take a lawsuit to free cell phone records and put people under oath to determine who had ordered the Hotshots out of the black. Sometimes truth was out of reach. I took their tree's wisdom to heart. I would wait.

December chill settled in on Prescott. My stint with the Forest Service ended somewhere between their six-month temp restrictions and Social Security's limit on how much money I could earn without being penalized. I would not return next year. The position had been eliminated, as firefighting needs engulfed the budget. I was considering Baja for the winter when my friend Jeffrey offered a vacated cottage on his land in Washington. He described a rural location on the 150-mile-long Skagit River. His land was a dozen miles from the zippy I-5 corridor on the edge of a bucolic farm valley. A good place to write. I'd not spent real time in the Pacific Northwest and I would be closer to Hope, who was finishing her Master's Degree in Eugene. I said yes. Jeffrey wanted to fly down and make the trip with me. I said yes again.

Goodbye, one more time, to landscape that nurtured me – sun and shadow on barren hills; cumulus clouds that exploded across the azure sky; the utter surprise of a Swainson's Hawk migration. I had rounded a curve on a narrow asphalt road and discovered a cast of hundreds. They had put down in a field to rest and feed; perched on every fencepost, in every sporadic tree. I watched through binocs, camera and tears. They took flight hours later, kettled up and up to reach the thermals that would carry them to their winter home in Argentina. Tens of thousands of these wayfaring hawks had recently been killed by the careless use of herbicides in Argentina. A sense of gloom permeated so many wild encounters.

We departed Prescott the second week of December. My desire to stop a few days in Joshua Tree National Park took us south before we headed west and north. South, into Yarnell. "Where the desert breeze meets the mountain air." My stomach turned; sadness cloaked my heart.

Charred houses dotted the boulder-clad hills. Turkey vultures frequented telephone poles. Handwritten signs declared businesses open, or hopeful plans to do so. I pulled over to take in the ash-covered mountain where the Hotshots had died. There, at the side of the road, a torrent of tears let loose for the men, their fatherless families and communities; for the unfinished tale that was Yarnell.

Grief and truth wove their own crying towel. As for grace, the ancient tree had already purveyed the answer.

Jeffrey and I were good travel buddies. Meaty philosophical conversation, only one argument over which way to turn (*just do as I say, will ya?*) and quick clarification on the platonic nature of our relationship. We stopped for two full-moon nights in Joshua Tree

National Park; dry camped at a deserted overlook at Mono Lake; watched otters play at a secluded boondock in northern California. We stretched the two lane highways as long as possible until forced to join the I-5 corridor in Oregon. Big box after big box, speed, lights … *What am I doing? I should be heading to Mexico.*

We arrived Sedro-Woolley on winter solstice. It was raining, of course. One of a thousand shades of gray. I pulled Perla to within ten feet of the steep bank that dropped down to the wide and forceful Skagit River. I was in earshot of the flow, tucked between the North Cascade Mountains and Puget Sound. Stunning Kulshan (Mt. Baker), a still-active volcano, loomed to the northeast. Thankfully, we were at the end of a dead-end road, quiet and dark. This could work. I planned a spring departure, three months of writing to finish the book. I headed for the casita that would be my new home; Jeffrey headed into his house. Friends, but no roof-raising benefits; smoke soon erupted from our separate woodstove chimneys.

The Skagit Valley was lush green and dreadfully damp. The temperate winter saw forty to fifty degree highs and the same range of lows. It was a psychic jolt to my thirty-five years in the southwest sun; another scale of wet from Montana. I'd traded Mexico's copper sunshine for the gray land of slugs. Sandstone for literal slick rock. Otters and seabirds took center stage with Siberia's wintering Trumpeter Swans. Dilapidated wooden barns dotted the landscape, artful beauties that hearkened back to my Iowa childhood. Birds and barns and three months; I would make every moment count. The 3:30 dusk had to be good for something.

I'd barely put pen to paper when I received word that Rick Steves' interview with me, taped months earlier, would be aired in

April. The radio show featured my New Mexico book and yikes! – the book was out of print. I'd let it disappear since photo scanning was not up to par. Now, photo technologies were improved. I jumped tracks from the writing project, retained the rights to *New Mexico's Sanctuaries, Retreats and Sacred Places* and set out to publish a new edition. I underestimated the mammoth task. New Mexico had a new area code. Every site in the book had to be checked and updated. I increased the number of photos by thirty, to over a hundred, which meant new layout. The book launched one week before the Easter-weekend interview aired.

My three-months' stay was up, I was exhausted and I'd done zilch on the book I'd planned to finish. I'd endured the misty winter and summer was around the bend. I shoved departure off the table; it was time to give my sun-starved soul a break. I hooked up with friends and kayaked island-dotted Puget Sound, the southern inland waters of the Salish Sea. We rubbed against rocky shores, caught high and low tides with variable success, picnicked and explored remote sandy beaches. Remote except for one, when I ambled over a knoll and surprised nude sunbathers on a gay beach. I froze as eight men looked up at once. Camera and binoculars around my neck, I gazed over them and out to sea, hoping, oh please, they grasped they were not my photographic intent.

A muscled, sun-bronzed Greek God rose from his blanket and swayed up the rocky mound to my perch. We locked eyes (*keep 'em high, Christina*) as he smiled welcome. I apologized for interrupting. He said no problem *go ahead and look around.* I did. I walked the intricate rock-lined paths, fire pits and altars they had created. Blue sea, white rocks, sinewy males, gardens ... imagine a nude beach painted by Maxfield Parrish. I was there.

When not looking west to the sea, I turned east and followed the Skagit River into the craggy peaks of North Cascades, into the utter stillness of the old growth cedar and Doug-fir forests. Not much old growth remained, and what did was fragmented. This destruction, along with the invasion of opportunistic and human-tolerant Barred Owls from the East, had caused the Spotted Owl's precarious existence. The age of their average nesting tree was 140 years. They preferred the weathered, fire-scarred giants that had loomed in arboreal communities for a thousand years – trunks where flying squirrels dwelled; where red voles tunneled through forest loam. The controversial struggle to save the owl went part and parcel with saving ancient forests. And beyond that, our souls. One Spotted Owl swoop through olden trees rendered us One.

What winter took away in mid-afternoon, summer gave back with her 10:00 p.m. twilight. I attended birding festivals. I rejoiced in sightings of Oystercatchers, seals, otters and Long-tailed Ducks. I hiked with Teak and Hobo along the poplar-treed dike that separated us from the Skagit River. Fawns and their mothers drank peacefully from ponds. Barred Owls hooted to mates. Otters gamboled on water-logged tree snags. Great Blue Herons lifted from still water to bullfrogs' croaky bass notes. And just when we settled to watch last light, a beaver tail slap startled serenity. Teak sprang to look over the riverbank and Hobo couldn't have cared less, content to let Teak take care of it.

Nature unfolded her mysteries with ease. Dating not so much. It was a conundrum, a mix that ranged from networking buddies – a newfound upshot of internet dating – and a few lovers.

I experienced my first *player,* a flashy white-haired dude from Orcas Island convinced he was Don Juan DeMarco. He wasn't. He was, however, a licensed coastguard captain who shouldn't have been, verified the day he steered inside a warning buoy at low tide and crashed a borrowed sailboat onto rocks. In Massacre Bay, no less. Across the boat I flew, through the galley door, wondering if the proverbial tunnel to the next life went past a kitchen sink. He righted the injured boat and I broke a left rib. He asked me to not tell a soul; embarrassed, he said. I guessed it had more to do with his Coast Guard license.

Boring? Not! I discovered – unearthed? – my first micro-penis; had a brief fling with a mailman who couldn't quite deliver and did some target shooting with a friend down by Yakima.

I liked Mr. Yakima. There was chemistry and we shared a love of solitude and intellect, but he turned out to be a bona fide member of the cult of measurement. He didn't make a move without ruminating for-EV-er. The spontaneity gene had skipped him. He, on the other hand, said I conducted my life by the seat of my pants, never a plan in place. He didn't mean it as a compliment. I gave him the moniker "Measured Man" and he called me "The Instigator." (To be continued.)

Sex after sixty? My pilot friend and I still banter over who tore whose clothes off first, mid-song, while fast-dancing in the living room. But overall, healthy, in-shape men with sexual staying power were a premium as aging figured into the mix. Many men bemoaned the unfairness, wondering why they penis-peaked at eighteen and post-meno women were frisky as ever. Nature's bum steer. And while several sister-friends over sixty settled for eunuch relationships (companionship but no sex) I held out for more. Intellect and play are important. So is chemistry. There is no need to settle. I love my own company. Most days it is all I can handle.

I took to dancing Sunday nights at the Old Edison Inn where the live music started at 5:30 and the community coalesced in song, conversation and laughs. Everyone danced. Rock, country, zydeco, swing – I chalked up the scene as a long gray day survival kit.

If black ice had an equivalent in the PNW, it was the slimy film that coated rocks. I was firing up to finish the book. I received the first edits August 2nd and planned to finish and depart by November. Friend Linda and I had kayaked to a distant island for lunch. The oft treacherous tide flows of Deception Pass were favorable on the blue-sky day as I kicked back in the kayak to watch dolphins skid by my paddles. We reached Deception Island and sought a sunny spot.

I decided to boulder up a few rocks; stepped back and planned my handholds. Six feet up I reached with my left arm and my right foot slipped. I dropped onto my right elbow with an electrifying crunch. My right arm pinned beneath my chest, I couldn't move. My standard lie-still-and-breathe-for-ten-minutes technique did not bring me back to normal. I pushed my arm to my side with excruciating pain. Nope. It wouldn't straighten. It was bad. Very. I managed to drop into the kayak, push off from shore and follow Linda across the Deception Pass currents.

Adrenaline is an amazing thing, flooding the body with strength to get us through crisis. I kept steely focus on the distant shoreline. I did not speak. My hand could barely hold the paddle but the arm garnered strength to stabilize the ten-foot craft. Three hours later the urgent care doctor walked toward me with x-rays.

*You kayaked back with **this**?*

He held up x-rays and pointed out two broken right ribs and the elbow. I'd broken off my crazy bone. Now there's a metaphor.

The only good thing about the ordeal, besides the Affordable Health Care Act, was a purple cast. I was right handed. I couldn't hold a pen or reach the computer keyboard to type. The book stopped as my stay stretched on. No way could I hook up Perla and head down the road. The universe forced a standstill.

The late summer days rolled into autumn and the sun went south. I pitifully pecked away with my left hand on the keyboard and opened a Facebook page for Hobo. I juiced up my music library, downloading tunes from the internet, something I'd wanted to do for years. I took long walks in the rain and danced, purple cast and all, at the Edison. But I didn't write, forced to trust the timing of what I could not see or understand.

My purple appendage cut away in October, I returned to the book. I was hell-bent to straighten my arm, despite the physical therapist who proclaimed he'd never seen an elbow as frozen as mine. Thank you very much. I switched to an occupational therapist as I headed into my second winter and developed a cough I could not shake, a hack from deep in my lungs, which brought out the worst in my broken ribs. I joked that moss grew in my lungs. Air temps weren't that cold but I could not get warm. My October birthday was a croupy affair with Linda and friends on La Conner's scenic wharf.

Around this time I received an email from Aunt Barb, Mom's younger sister. Aunt Barb was eighty-two. She and Mom resided in Iowa and lived within twenty miles of each other. I didn't normally communicate with Aunt Barb so her email was a surprise. She wanted to know if I had heard of Nora May, my great-grandmother on my mother's side. I'd never heard her name mentioned. Ever.

Included in the email was a photo of an angelic teenager with thick brown braids. There was no smile. Her demeanor relayed an inquisitive spirit; a profound and serious inner strength. She could have been a young queen. *This is Nora May, the mother of your grandma*

Velva wrote Barb ... *too bad us kids did not inherit her lovely hair. I will send you a story about her soon.*

Another email arrived the next day:

Tonight is one of those sleepless ones for me so i thought it a good time to write you about your great grandmother. Mom stopped me one morning just as i was about to leave for school ... Out of nowhere she told me that years before her dad had shot and killed her mother.

I was spellbound.

Aunt Barb began the search for Nora May's secreted life after her mother died. She turned first to her ninety-year- old Aunt Dollie, Nora May's only surviving child. She was a toddler when her mother was killed and remembered only bits of information. She recalled May was named for her May Day birthday. She played organ at church on Sundays. Most intriguing of all, she accompanied silent movies on the piano at the local theatre. Despite dreadful abuse and poverty, May found outlet for her creative spirit. My muse was born of hers. And so was Aunt Barb's: she was the silent poet of the family.

Although she recalled little, Aunt Dollie gave Barb permission to tell May's story. Barb and daughters made sojourns to the pastoral cemetery on the edge of West Liberty to find her grave. After several failed attempts, one exciting day they scraped away the dirt between May's parents' graves and discovered a tiny stone. Certain of success, they returned with tracing paper and scribbled over the script with soft lead pencil, but they could not decipher what weather and time had erased.

Aunt Barb was undaunted. A manila envelope arrived in my mailbox with a folded photocopy of a newspaper account from November 1917. I devoured the words, shocked to discover May's murder happened on Thanksgiving Day. Her final hours unfolded in a flourish of flowery prose (from the *Muscatine Journal,* typos included):

> ***Liberty Man Shoots Wife Kills Self:*** *Breaking into the basement of his own home last night, Albert Dunlap at 7 o'clock this morning brought a sordid drama of domestic unhappiness to a culumination in a flash of vivid tragedy when he murdered his wife, May Dunlap, who was sueing him for a divorce, and turned his revolver against himself dying instantly.*
>
> *Dunlap was sent down to the Muscatine county jail some weeks ago on a thirty day sentence for intoxication as a result of charges brought by Mrs. Dunlap. It was alleged that returning to his home after a drunken orgy Dunlap burned the furniture and otherwise ran amuck.*
>
> *After Dunlap had been brought to Muscatine Mrs. Dunlap filed a suit for divorce alleging that for two years the husband had been drinking to excess. It was alleged that Dunlap was quarrelsome and cruel and that while under the influence of drink he addressed himself to his wife and children in improper terms and that upon one occasion he bent her over a chair.*

My great-grandmother must have been as determined as she was fearful the day she had filed charges, three years before women were granted the right to vote. She didn't know how the police would respond; if they would protect her in a time when men ruled the households.

May was taken seriously. Albert was removed from the house and incarcerated. Jailers noted Dunlap was in a constant state of agitation, pacing in his cell. He wrote letters to May threatening to kill her, yet he was released after his thirty-day sentence. He hopped a train for his mother's home and retrieved his gun. From there he departed for West Liberty, fifty miles away. Local officers were on the lookout for him at the depot but he swung off the slow-moving train a block from home, broke through the basement window and waited overnight with his .22-calibre Colt.

I wonder. Did May awaken to an Indian summer morning that fated day in the Iowa heartland? Was she wearing her favorite calico dress as she brushed her children's hair? Did she sing, or did she fidget as she fought to ignore her husband's threats? Her mother-in-law was with her in the kitchen where they dressed two chickens for the meager holiday meal.

> *This morning Mrs. Dunlap, following a custom made necessary by years of hard work supporting a family of children as well as a husband whose habits prevented his holding a steady job, arose early and went about her labors. After she had been at work for some time she took a coal scuttle and went to the basement to secure coal for the kitchen stove. She had gotten almost to the coal pile when she observed Dunlap rise out of the corner and come toward her. The frightened woman turned and ran "He's come after me."*
>
> *... Mrs. Dunlap though mortally wounded staggered away from Dunlap and apparently the man believing his work not yet done, again seized and again holding her fired a second missle through the dying woman's temple.*

May had placed her love for her children above all else. She was a heroine, but back then, she was buried and wiped from memory in the name of family shame, her existence whispered in rare moments.

I could understand that secretive choices were made. But shame for Albert Dunlap should no longer translate into Nora May's desertion. She'd heard the *SNAP!* and acted against all odds. If I had known about May I would have named my daughter after her. Nora May was buried once in the ground and a second time in memory. A few of us vowed her memory would rise.

Aunt Barb passed Aunt Dollie's consent to tell Nora May's story to me. I penned a short essay to honor May's spirit on the Day of the Dead when those who have died are acknowledged. Cultural customs vary: some prepare the dead's favorite food while others construct altars of remembrance; pull out a bottle of their favorite spirits and have a good talk. I broke May's story in a short blog on November 3rd, 2014. It felt like the perfect time.

One week later I received an email from my mother, irate that I had written about Nora May. She ordered me to *delete it at once or do not expect to ever hear from me again.*

Reality flipped, a pitchpole of the human kind. Minutes, hours and days beyond found me heartsick and mad, defiant and perplexed. Mom had cast a *Sophie's Choice* ultimatum. She forced me to choose between my great-grandmother and her; and between myself as daughter or writer. This was the stuff of myth and Shakespeare.

My mom: Margaret Lucille. She knew Aunt Barb was seeking information on Nora May: Aunt Barb had approached her but she sluffed it off. I responded to Mom's email, outlining the search and permissions given. I apologized for her upset, at a loss to understand her fury. I couldn't help but wonder if this was really about Nora May.

A decade earlier I had unearthed the story of my father's mother and grandmother in Denmark. It involved a child out of wedlock and an intriguing tale of survival. Once I returned to Iowa, my slideshow and subsequent story were celebrated by the family. I had anticipated a similar response.

I suggested we talk. She did not respond. Unless you count unfriending me on Facebook.

According to Nancy, my Swinomish Native American friend, acknowledging May was crucial. Because she was murdered and hidden away, her spirit would not rest until recognized. Hope, Aunt Barb, her daughters, granddaughters and I held a commemoration for May on Thanksgiving morning. Hope and I in Washington and they in Iowa, we timed our tributes to take place simultaneously as we lit candles and paid homage to the spirited woman at the Wurlitzer. We gave voice to her valor and sacrifice. She, our pioneer megastar. Our super slice of DNA.

Soon thereafter May came to Hope in a dream. She stepped hesitantly out of dark shadows in a dusty basement. She wore a dirty white shirt tucked into a long white skirt. She took Hope's hand and taught her how to dance.

Mom has not replied to notes or emails. She sends no birthday wishes; she has disappeared from my life. There are moments when I wish she'd die so I could like her again. I see Nora May's hard-working qualities in my mom. I believe she would have responded similarly on behalf of her children. Well, maybe not me.

I hear her say *It's been a slice.*

I moved the good memories of Mom to the forefront. Her fierceness. Her little body that produces its own head of steam. I won't forget the day we drove along a lonely Colorado highway and she pointed out a tree snag on a distant hill. It stood alone, and in a moment of grace she shared her awe. Years later she would hand me a copy of *The Bridges of Madison County.* The only book she ever gave me, it is a tale of unrequited love. There is no greater grief than that of love unanswered.

We become the stories we do not tell. We kick shame in the shins when we do.

I sat at river's edge. A Bald Eagle delivered a salmon to her newly-fledged eaglet on the sandbar. She coaxed her young into shallow waters to eat as the mate swooped in. The three eagles hopped and chirped; fulfilled the miracle of continuation as I struggled to comprehend the recent events. I had asked for a break from book pressures and received my first-ever broken bones. They forced me to stop and stay; positioned me to receive the story of Nora May. May's entry into my life was the event the numen had foretold; the familial karmic knots of Carole's mountaintop Tarot reading that culminated in the ancient juniper's portending words: There was no grace without truth.

Quest is the art of discovery through serendipity. Serendipity isn't dumb luck. The serendipitous person pays attention to what she encounters, gathers information through all senses, perceives vibrations and links so-called coincidences together. According to one researcher, people fall into one of three groups. The non-encounterers rarely stray from to-do lists. Occasional encounterers infrequently stumble into serendipity. The third and smallest group were super-encounterers, who see surprises everywhere. I was straight off the Isle of Serendip.

Five years into my quest I'd floated SE, pushed up dirt roads and motored down asphalt. Now I was becalmed on the watery wild Skagit. Like a magician whose movement went unnoticed, the deeply flowing river had changed me. While her chinook, silvers, chums, pinks and sockeye had splashed, swum and leaped their way upstream, She-river had smoothed rough, impatient edges and sculpted me anew.

I had stared rapt at spring floods, watching her morph into a horizontal forest of torn trees. I'd kayaked her curves with friends, past tree snag walls three stories high, spawning dreams of Godzilla-sized beavers. Trickster coyote had watched from the bank as kayak-amiga Linda followed me into a ninety-degree turn at a confluence of two creeks. Her kayak tipped and she was seized by a deadhead and pulled under. I watched helplessly until she popped up like a bobber, drenched, chilled and shaken on the other side of the snag.

Confluence: the literal and metaphorical merging of breathtaking forces.

Swift waters mold spirit. Strong curves change the course of life. The Skagit's Black-headed Grosbeak, Yellow Warbler and chirpy Cedar Waxwing were daily callers; Chestnut-backed Chickadees delivered a morning song. I charted the seasons by the sun's rise along her ribbon of wet, the only view line I had in the land of tall trees.

Yes, the Skagit was a generous one. As part of the Wild and Scenic River system, she wound through the Cascades and emptied onto fertile farmlands below, growing organic food for thought, body and spirit. Her floodplain was one of the richest in the world. Her delta blossomed in winter with thousands of Snow Geese; spring fields erupted into dazzling tulip fields, vivid red and yellow strips.

Now, her low waters were the warmest on record. Neighbor Vern, from a four-generation farm family, said he'd never seen the river so shallow. Salmon were undersized. *It's as if they are returning early from the sea before they mature* said Native fisherwoman Nancy. I watched as they splashed at the entrance to dry spawning streams.

They waited for rain; for the flow to return. For humans to grasp the havoc we wreak.

Teak, Hobo and I walked along the dike. Rain was projected to fall for six days. A black and white Bald soared up behind me at tree height; disappeared with a remarkable cry. Within seconds her full-sized brown juvenile glided overhead through low light and landed on a nearby limb. This closeness was new. Then again, I'd been there for a year and a half. I'd watched them fledge, grow and eat salmon on sand bars. They recognized me.

Well hello I said, and began to cry. *Yes, I see you. You are beautiful beyond words. I'm sorry your river is warm; that your salmon struggle.* The young eagle looked down, as if he understood every word, yielding not blame or pardon. Teak and Hobo stood dead still. I wanted to ask forgiveness, but the words stuck in my throat. How does one ask forgiveness for altering the web of life? *I love you* I said.

I put my hand over my heart and nodded goodnight. Teak and Hobo followed close beside as I walked slowly to Perla. There was a different sound to the Skagit. A new rapid had formed as her waters grew shallower.

There are too damned many of us.

I vowed to be in a quaking aspen forest for autumn – to lie on my back, watch the dizzy shimmer of leaves against the southwest cerulean sky. My lungs craved arid. I longed for sharp-edged mountaintop clarity found only above timberline, like the Sharkstooth Pass I'd left so long ago.

Yes, landscape mattered. It affected me in distinct ways. Writing didn't come as easy in the Pacific Northwest. My brain took longer to find the precise word. My body was more sluggish at sea level. I sensed an invisible cap on spiritual highs.

Mauve skies captivated in their own soft way, but my weathered Georgia O'Keeffe face was an outcast in these damp lands, where women barely suffered crow's feet. My skin yearned to be brown again. Even the owls were grayer, as their relatives to the south boasted brown. I poured vinegar into a bucket of water and set up the step ladder. It was time to scrub the moss off Perla, as my mind commenced to chatter.

What if I arrived in Arizona and the sun stung? What if New Mexico's shadow-brilliant light ceased to amaze? Might I pine for a cloudy veil, the emerald lush? I would miss dancing to the Bow Diddlers. Fresh fried oysters. Of course I would. Once southbound, I knew not how the scales would tip. This, however, I did know: no decision was permanent to one who lived a good death. There were no wrong turns. U-turns were You-turns that erupted in unforeseen mercies and contradiction. To get lost was to be found. Dead ends were beginnings. Every sign pointed home in invisible ink.

Home is a house, a town, a piece of land. Home means family, the place where a lover waits, where best friends dwell. My home is Perla, a hitchhiking cat and a tail-wagging Lab. Home is where I hang the birdfeeder; touch the eons-old gastrolith that sits upon my altar. Home is my scarlet pen and a journal at hand. Home is Hope in my heart. When I drop the trappings and pare away place, however, home is I AM. There are no walls. No closets contain ghosts. No basement door blocks fear. Heartache is not stuffed in a box, secreted away in an attic next to the famished shadows of grief.

I AM is renewal, not an analytical upgrade. A pulsating spiral passage into unknown realms, not a flowchart. I AM is the wild road home.

Epilogue

Hobo looked askew as I slipped the harness around his belly and neck. It was time to hit the road. I loaded Teak and we intrepid three were southwest bound. That night, on the banks of the Willamette River, I dreamed of a rock edifice that jutted from a tall mountain. That is all. No message, no directions, just the brilliant stalwart.

We boondocked lakeside in exhilarating sleet near Oregon's Sisters. Into Nevada we rolled, across cloudstruck horizons into the endless, deserted plains of Great Basin National Park. Hobo traipsed up and down the hoodoos of Utah's Goblin Valley, our final desert stay before climbing into the aspen-coated mountains of Colorado. I made it just in time: peak color on Fall Equinox. I breathed deep and clear again. I plopped down on my back and made leaf angels of crackling gold. Laughed hysterically as Teak licked my face.

When friends inquired about winter plans my best answer was *southern Arizona.* I would continue down the highway by Measured Man's "seat of my pants." I smiled, thinking of his recent text and news of his epiphanies. He'd decided to quit his school administration job, sell his house, buy an RV and trade the town car for a pickup. He still held the ruler but his fifty-nine-year-old grip gave way. The Instigator winked.

I drove the I-19 toward Nogales; came up on the exit for Arivaca Road and there it was, eee-yi! the rock edifice I had dreamed. I exited, literally following my dreams. The rough asphalt two-lane rolled with the contours of the earth, made sinewy turns across swaying grasslands and thornbush, reminiscent of the Serengeti Plain. My eyes searched for a loping giraffe.

I steered onto a hilltop pullout. Teak's ears perked up in anticipation. *Best dog in the world.* We jumped from the truck and I opened the door for Hobo. The air was crystal dry. I slowly exhaled as euphoria and fatigue of years on the road came to bear. Cotton ball clouds formed aerial stepping stones west to Baboquivari Peak, the granite monolith sacred to the Tohono O'odham. This was jaguar land. Their Tikal spirits imbued the air; mud-soft footsteps lined mountain streams.

All was sky in this place of space. Primordial potential that spoke to creation itself; summoned every electron to a fiery I AM sweat-and-sinew-dance. The drumbeat must persist. The heart of human fate is startlingly simple: safeguard the wild, and in so doing, we save ourselves and our hallowed planet home.

Hobo rubbed against my leg and moved on to nudge Teak's chin.

A sudden breeze whispered through my hair. I answered *Yes.*

② Acknowledgements

Special thanks to Emilie Vardaman, editor, for her indefatigable work, feedback and patience.

Thank you Kizzen Lakai, my take-no-prisoners substantive editor and cover maven.

Thanks Jeanne Combo for tireless feedback and keeping my boat jargon honest. Thanks to readers Hope Nealson, Amy Schleier and Carole Summer.

Thank you Debora Lewis, indie formatter through thick and thin.

Thanks Beau Bailey for the maps; Bob Giles for ventures into your Utah homeland that gleaned the cover of this book.

Thanks to the labyrinth makers for graciously sharing your sacred circles. Trains and all.

Thanks to friends along the road with places to park, meals, hikes and bathtubs of love. Jeffrey Isbrandtsen for my Skagit River home. Lee Hester for spirit-soothing massage. Julianne Buskirk and Philip Walters for protective storage space. Danielle Desruisseaux, keeper of the Kerastan. Heartfelt gratitude to Aunt Barb DeGood for guiding me to Nora May, the place where words fail.

Thanks to wild men and guy guides, fierce moments and luscious repose.

Thank you Sisters, heroic women who, like the mighty bison, face the storms and walk through; who dream the wild road home.

About the Author

Christina Nealson is the author of five books and photographer of four. Photojournalist assignments have taken her to Africa, Central America and throughout the West, from Alaska to the tip of the Baja. She winters in the southwest and is a interpretive park ranger in the summer. Her honors include finalist for the Colorado Book Award, Quill Award finalist (La Femme de Prose Books) and *Focus on Women Magazine* Author of the Year. Her travel companions are Teak the Lab and Hobo the marmalade adventure cat. On the road for thirteen years, she senses change a comin'.

www.christinanealson.com

View slideshow for *Wild Road Home!*

Praise for *Wild Road Home*

"*Wild Road Home* is a loving paean to the natural world, to the wonders of the country we live in, and to a peripatetic soul seeking a grail that she often finds in many different wild places... and then moves on. The journey is fascinating and never really ends. One is reminded that the greatest journey is usually to be found in the spirit and in the mind."

– John Nichols, author of
The Milagro Beanfield War
and *My Heart Belongs to Nature*

"Christina Nealson writes about the American West with poetic imagery, grit, and compassion. She fully realizes what's at stake here – not just the continued existence of dynamic species and sacred places, but also our very humanity and last vestiges of sanity."

– Stephen Jones, co-founder, Boulder Rights of Nature; author of
The Last Prairie,
Peterson Field Guide to the North American Prairie,
Colorado Nature Almanac and
Butterflies of the Colorado Front Range

"Utterly courageous, Christina dares to do what we would do, were it not for fear. Safe, dry, warm and comfortable, we trek with her once again in *Wild Road Home,* jaws agape over her sensuous, amazing and sometimes hair-raising expeditions from Alaska to Mexico. Of course, there are tantalizing, sexy men who promise much, drink to excess, and have skills and wild places to share. Ultimately – other than Christina's unconquerable spirit – the only constants in her quest are Blue the truck, La Perla the trailer, Teak the "best dog in the world," and a Grandmother Tree. The home she seeks is just around the bend, and in the hearts of all who would dare to learn, love and have the courage to share."

– Charlene Baldridge, author of
The Warriors' Duet, The Rose in December
and *San Diego Diego, Jewel of the California Coast*

"Christina Nealson is a storyteller of the highest caliber. You're bound to think of rough and tumble Edward Abbey, but in her latest book, *Wild Road Home,* Christina writes from the heart as a sensitive, observant lover of nature. The outdoors serve as her spiritual guide, and the imagery of her narrative writing is as vivid as photography. This self-described "womad" (woman nomad) shares her travels, her joys, and her sadness. Each page is a lesson in self-discovery and resilience that both women and men can relish and learn from."

– Jack Challem, author of
The Inflammation Syndrome and *No More Fatigue*

"Wild road, indeed! When you travel with Christina Nealson, keep your seatbelt fastened. It's pedal to the metal and don't look back!"

– William deBuys, author of
The Last Unicorn

"Christina Nealson's raw and spirit-affirming memoir makes you yearn to go beyond the safety of your comfortable life and meet the world with open-eyed wonder. Eloquent and down to earth, *Wild Road Home* bespeaks a woman's courage, freedom and commitment to craft. Take your place in the passenger seat as Nealson unfurls a passionate, perilous quest to find the meaning of home."

– Ginny Williams, Career & Executive Coach

Granite Mountain's Alligator Juniper

there is no grace without truth